MW01240725

ANCHORED
HOPE
IN

BE STILL . . .

LET YOUR HEART SPEAK

AN ALPHABETICAL ANTHOLOGY

MARGUERITE PATRICIA GILNER

COPYRIGHT © 2022 BY MARGUERITE PATRICIA GILNER. ALL RIGHTS RESERVED. NO PART OF THIS PUBLICATION MAY BE REPRODUCED OR TRANSMITTED IN ANY FORM OR BY ANY MEANS, ELECTRONIC, MECHANICAL, PHOTOCOPYING, RECORDING, OR OTHERWISE, WITHOUT PRIOR WRITTEN PERMISSION OF THE AUTHOR.

PRINTED IN THE UNITED STATES OF AMERICA.

SCRIPTURE QUOTATIONS ARE FROM THE NEW REVISED STANDARD VERSION BIBLE: CATHOLIC EDITION, (NRSV) COPYRIGHT © 1989, 1993 BY THE NATIONAL COUNCIL OF THE CHURCHES OF CHRIST IN THE UNITED STATES OF AMERICA. USED BY PERMISSION. CREDITS ACKNOWLEDGED WITH OTHER QUOTATIONS.

GENRE: *SPIRITUALITY, PSYCHOLOGY, QUALITY OF LIFE*

AUTHOR: GILNER, MARGUERITE PATRICIA, AUTHOR, 1942-
TITLE: *ANCHORED IN HOPE: BE STILL . . . LET YOUR HEART SPEAK*

COVER DESIGN: MARGUERITE PATRICIA GILNER
INTERIOR DESIGN AND PHOTOGRAPHIC ART: MARGUERITE PATRICIA GILNER

ISBN: (HARDCOVER) 979-8-4167110-4-7

ISBN: (PAPERBACK) 979-8-4146125-3-7

LIBRARY OF CONGRESS CONTROL NUMBER: 2022903627

AUTHOR'S EMAIL ADDRESS: <u>SEASIDERETREAT@COMCAST.NET</u>   041722..1

A gift from the heart

To:

From:

Wishing you an ocean of blessings!

In the midst of winter,
I have discovered
within me
an invincible spring
filled with

RENEWED HOPE.

Albert Camus

Adapted by Marguerite P. Gilner

Dedication

In loving memory of

my dear sister, Ann.

I have an ocean of cherished memories,
warming my heart until we meet again.

And in gratitude to

Judi and Linda

two dear friends and former high school students
for their tender loving outreach
during the most difficult time
of my cancer journey.
They were a gift and a blessing,
helping me to be anchored in HOPE.

Table of Contents

Life

"Life is an opportunity, benefit from it.

Life is a beauty, admire it.

Life is bliss, taste it.

Life is a dream, realize it.

Life is a challenge, meet it.

Life is a duty, complete it.

Life is a game, play it.

Life is costly, care for it.

Life is wealth, keep it.

Llife is love, enjoy it.

Life is mystery, know it.

Life is a promise, fulfill it.

Life is a sorrow, overcome it.

Life is a song, sing it.

Life is a struggle, accept it.

Life is a tragedy, confront it.

Life is an adventure, dare it.

Life is luck, make it.

Life is too precious, do not destroy it.

Life is Life, fight for it!."

Mother Teresa of Calcutta

HOPE
the heartbeat of the Soul

Preface

THE RESILIENCE
OF THE HUMAN SPIRIT

THE HISTORY OF OUR ANCESTORS REMINDS US OF THE RESILIENCE OF THE HUMAN SPIRIT. RECORDED STORIES SHARE ACCOUNTS OF COURAGE AND SURVIVAL DURING THE MOST DEVASTATING TIMES. *ANCHORED IN HOPE* IS AN OUTGROWTH OF A CONVICTION THAT OUR SPIRITUAL BELIEFS, AFFIRMATIONS, AND POSITIVE THINKING CAN HELP SUSTAIN US DURING CHALLENGING TIMES. THE COVID-19, CAUSING A PANDEMIC, TOOK US BY SURPRISE. THREE YEARS LATER, WE ARE STILL ADAPTING TO A NEW NORMAL. IT CHANGED OUR WAY OF BEING, INTRODUCING US TO AN ELEMENT OF FEAR, UNLIKE ANYTHING WE EVER EXPERIENCED. AS WE SLOWED DOWN AND STAYED HOME, WE HAD TIME TO REFLECT ON THE MEANING AND PURPOSE OF OUR LIVES' JOURNEYS. NOW, IN OUR THIRD YEAR, WE LOOK BACK WITH A FEELING

OF RELIEF AND A SENSE OF HOPE. AS WE REVIEWED THE HAPPENINGS OF THE PAST SEVERAL YEARS, A FAVORABLE OUTCOME CAME IN THE INNER STRENGTH WE GAINED. IT GAVE US THE COURAGE TO SEEK A BETTER *QUALITY OF LIFE*, EVEN DURING UNUSUAL CIRCUMSTANCES. FEAR AND MYSTERY CREATED A PANIC THAT TOOK SOME OF US TO A VULNERABLE PLACE, QUESTIONING OUR LIFE'S PURPOSE. IT CHALLENGED US TO SLOW DOWN AND BE STILL, TO RELY ON OUR INNER STRENGTH, AND LIVE IN THE PRESENT, APPRECIATING THE GIFT OF TODAY.

THIS BOOK'S REFLECTIONS PROVIDE INSIGHT AND THOUGHT-PROVOKING OPPORTUNITIES ON ESSENTIAL PRINCIPLES WE VALUE AND PRACTICE. WHILE WRITING, I RECOGNIZED A PATTERN WAS UNFOLDING WITH THEMES THAT COVERED MOST OF THE ALPHABET. I TOOK THAT CONCEPT AND CREATED AN ALPHABETICAL ANTHOLOGY OF REFLECTIONS TO CHALLENGE AND MOTIVATE US TO SEEK ANSWERS TO THE QUESTIONS WE PONDER. WRITING *ANCHORED IN HOPE* HAS CHALLENGED ME TO REFLECT ON THE IMPORTANT VALUES I HOLD DEAR. I HOPE THE REFLECTIONS WILL LEND INSIGHT AND SHED UNDERSTANDING TO GIVE YOU A GREATER SENSE OF YOUR UNIQUENESS AS YOU FIND SOLACE AND PEACE.

AS WE IMAGINE A FUTURE FILLED WITH HOPE, IMAGES OF THE PANDEMIC AND OTHER PERSONAL STRUGGLES ARE FRESH ON OUR MINDS. WE DON'T WANT TO RETURN TO A PRE-PANDEMIC STATE BUT HOPE TO GO FORWARD AND APPRECIATE LIVING A MORE INTENTIONAL LIFESTYLE.

ONE OF THE POSITIVE OUTCOMES OF THE PANDEMIC WAS HAVING THE GIFT OF TIME TO SLOW DOWN, BE STILL, AND TAKE NOTICE OF OUR HECTIC LIVES. FOR SOME, THE QUARANTINE BECAME A TIME OF DISCERNMENT, AS WE SOUGHT AFTER A SPIRITUAL QUEST. THIS QUEST BROUGHT US TO A FORK IN THE ROAD, AWARE THAT OUR DECISIONS DETERMINE THE DIRECTION AND LIFESTYLE WE CHOOSE. HOW WE LIVE, WHAT WE BELIEVE, AND HOW WE RELATE TO THOSE WHO ACCOMPANY US DETERMINE THE CHOICES WE MAKE. IN THE PROCESS, OUR INNER RESILIENCE UNVEILS STRENGTHS UNIMAGINED UNTIL TESTED. SAYING *"YES"* TO ONE PATH IS SAYING *"NO"* TO OTHER PATHS. HARVEY COX TELLS US, *"NOT TO DECIDE IS TO DECIDE."* WE ARE ALWAYS MAKING DECISIONS, EVEN WHEN WE DECIDE NOT TO DECIDE.

SOME DISCOVERED NEW GIFTS AND TALENTS DURING THE STAY HOME PHASE. SOME FOUND NEW HOPE, AND SOME EXPERIENCED GREATER PEACE BY OPTING FOR A

SIMPLER, LESS COMPLICATED LIFESTYLE. SADLY, MANY EXPERIENCED HEARTACHES AND LOSSES THAT WERE UNEXPECTED. SOME, MORE THAN OTHERS, SUFFERED ENORMOUS LOSSES, INCLUDING THE DEATH OF LOVED ONES AND FRIENDS. COVID-19 WILL GO DOWN IN HISTORY AS A TIME THAT BROUGHT US TO OUR KNEES. NEVERTHELESS, OUR RESILIENT SPIRIT SOUGHT A PEACEFUL CALM WHILE LIVING WITH THE UNCERTAINTY OF THIS TRAGEDY.

AS I PEN THIS PREFACE ON EASTER SUNDAY, MY HEART REJOICES WITH HOPEFULNESS. HOPE IS ON THE HORIZON. SPRING IS EVIDENT, WITNESSED BY TINY BUDS APPEARING ON THE BARREN BRANCHES. THE DELICATE CROCI AND SUN-KISSED DAFFODILS SPRING UP THROUGH THE RECENTLY THAWED EARTH. THESE IMAGES ANNOUNCE A TIME OF REBIRTH, A NEW BEGINNING. OUR HOPEFULNESS EMERGES AS WE LISTEN TO OUR HEARTS AND PAY ATTENTION TO OUR NEEDS AND DESIRES. LISTEN, YOUR HEART HOLDS THE ANSWERS TO THE QUESTIONS YOU PONDER. BE COURAGEOUS AND ACT ACCORDINGLY.

I HOPE YOU WILL TAKE THE TIME TO BE STILL AND CONTEMPLATE WHAT IS IMPORTANT TO YOU AND USE THE JOURNAL PAGES TO JOT DOWN YOUR PERSONAL INSIGHTS AND PERCEPTIONS. DO NOT GIVE YOUR YESTERDAYS THE POWER TO DEFINE YOUR TOMORROWS. YOU WRITE YOUR OWN STORY, ONE CHAPTER AT A TIME.

FROM THIS DAY FORWARD, MAY YOUR LIFE BE A STORY OF RESILIENCE, OPTIMISM, GRATITUDE, AND JOY!

HAPPY EASTER! WISHING YOU BLESSINGS FILLED WITH RENEWED HOPE AND PEACE.

TAKE GENTLE CARE.

Marguerite Patricia Gilner

EASTER SUNDAY, APRIL 17, 2022
MILTON, DELAWARE

And the People Stayed Home

Kitty O'Meara

(PRINTED WITH PERMISSION.)

AND THE PEOPLE STAYED HOME.

AND READ BOOKS AND LISTENED, AND RESTED AND EXERCISED.

AND MADE ART AND PLAYED GAMES,

AND LEARNED NEW WAYS OF BEING AND WERE STILL,

AND LISTENED MORE DEEPLY.

SOME MEDITATED, SOME PRAYED, SOME DANCED.

SOME MET THEIR SHADOWS.

AND THE PEOPLE BEGAN TO THINK DIFFERENTLY.

AND THE PEOPLE HEALED.

AND IN THE ABSENCE OF PEOPLE LIVING IN IGNORANT,

DANGEROUS, MINDLESS AND HEARTLESS WAYS

THE EARTH BEGAN TO HEAL.

AND WHEN THE DANGER PASSED,

AND THE PEOPLE JOINED TOGETHER AGAIN,

THEY GRIEVED THEIR LOSSES, AND MADE NEW CHOICES,

AND DREAMED NEW IMAGES,

AND CREATED NEW WAYS TO LIVE AND HEAL THE EARTH FULLY,

AS THEY HAD BEEN HEALED.

Prologue

"HOPE IS THE HEARTBEAT OF THE SOUL."

With hope in our hearts, we can weather the emotionally and mentally challenging storms that come our way and live to see a beautiful sunrise welcoming a new day. Since I was a young adult, the word *"HOPE"* has been my mantra. It is a powerful word because of all it implies. I have used the word *HOPE* as part of my passwords, access codes on bank accounts, locks, and computers. I am unsure when *HOPE* became meaningful to me, but it dates back to my early twenties. Hope has been a powerful force in helping me survive significant challenges. Blessed with a positive and hopeful attitude, I have survived unusual crises on several occasions. No matter how bleak a situation, I believed that in the end, I would bounce back. Remarkably, bouncing back has been a welcomed occurrence throughout my life.

My analogy of hope is that of a breeze. You can feel a breeze but not see it. A breeze is invisible to the eye but gentle to our somatosensory perception that refreshes our being. So, also with the concept of hope. Hope has the quality that boosts our spirits and gives us the courage to work through a process to survive the difficult times. Without hope, we are void of the courage to fight the good fight.

I was diagnosed with advanced-stage ovarian cancer in my thirties. The diagnosis came on the heels of a three-month hospitalization with endocarditis. My poor prognosis devastated me. The chemotherapy treatments were for palliative care to buy me some time, not to cure. After being discharged from the hospital from my first surgery, I wanted something tangible, a visible reminder to be hopeful, trust in God, and believe in miracles. I went to a jewelry store in downtown Baltimore a few blocks from where I lived, searching for an anchor to wear as a necklace. I found one that seemed perfect, but it was too expensive. I kept revisiting the jewelry store and checking to see if it was still there. The store owner was an elderly gentleman who observed my frequent visits and finally asked me why I was interested in the anchor necklace. I told him about my diagnosis and how I wanted to wear an anchor I could cling to as my sign of hope. He offered me a deal: He would reduce the price if I prayed for him (he was also battling cancer). We had an agreement, and I left the store wearing the anchor necklace. I only took it off when I was in surgery. It was a tangible sign that accompanied me through my many hospitalizations, chemotherapy treatments, and subsequent surgery visits. Forty years later, I still wear the anchor necklace as a visible sign of hope and a reminder of my remarkable healing.

> In the end, it is not the years in your life that counts. It's the life in your years.
> *Abraham Lincoln*

As I worked on this book's design, I incorporated the anchor's image with daffodils and fresh falling snow to symbolize the mystery and power

OF HOPEFULNESS. THE ANCHOR, A CHRISTIAN SYMBOL OF HOPE, REPRESENTS THE STABILITY THAT KEEPS US FROM DRIFTING AIMLESSLY. THE DAFFODIL SURVIVES THE LATE WINTER SNOWFALL TO BLOSSOM INTO A VIBRANT SPRING FLOWER. AND SNOW HAS A MAGICAL QUALITY, FALLING SOFTLY AND GRACEFULLY, BLANKETING THE LANDSCAPE WITH A GLISTENING GLOW. I HAVE INCORPORATED THESE IMAGES TO CREATE A DESIGN THAT, FOR ME, EPITOMIZES RENEWED HOPE.

AS I GET OLDER, I APPRECIATE THE IMPORTANCE OF SLOWING DOWN AND BEING STILL. IT IS CHALLENGING FOR ME TO QUIET MYSELF FROM ALL DISTRACTIONS AND LISTEN TO MY HEART. WHEN I DO, I CAN FOCUS ON WHAT REALLY MATTERS. JACK KORNFIELD RELATES, *"PART OF THE ART OF QUIETING YOURSELF IS ALSO TO HONOR THE TEARS THAT YOU CARRY."* TEARS ARE PART OF MY JOURNEY, AND YOURS, TOO. ACKNOWLEDGING OUR PAIN AIDS IN HEALING THE HURTS THAT HAVE LEFT THE SCARS. MY FAITH GIVES ME TO STRENGTH TO CARRY ON. POPE FRANCIS REMINDS US, *"HAVING FAITH DOES NOT MEAN HAVING NO DIFFICULTIES, BUT HAVING THE STRENGTH TO FACE THEM, KNOWING WE ARE NOT ALONE."*

THE CORONAVIRUS HAS IMPACTED OUR LIVES AND CHANGED OUR CONCEPT OF NORMALCY. IT CAME WITHOUT NOTICE, AND THEN SUDDENLY, COVID-19 CHALLENGED US TO LIVE LIFE DIFFERENTLY. MANY THOUGHT IT WAS ONLY FOR A FEW WEEKS OR A MONTH, BUT IT HAS BEEN MORE THAN A YEAR OF SOCIAL DISTANCING, WEARING MASKS, AND STAYING HOME. AND, WE HAVE DISCOVERED THINGS ABOUT OURSELVES WE NEVER IMAGINED.

THE ISOLATION GAVE US AN INVITATION TO LOOK INWARD AND QUESTION OUR PRIORITIES AND VALUES. OUR HOPE IS REAL, EVEN THOUGH WE ARE FRUSTRATED AND EXHAUSTED WITH ALL THE RESTRICTIONS AND FEARS OF THE UNKNOWNS. WE DREAM OF THE TIME THERE WILL BE NO RESTRICTIONS, WHEN WE CAN FREELY HUG AGAIN, EMBRACE THOSE WE LOVE, ENJOY FRIENDSHIPS, AND CELEBRATE SPECIAL TIMES. WE HAVE LEARNED TO SEEK BALANCE THROUGH IT ALL AND TO BE PATIENT AS WE AWAIT SOME RESEMBLANCE OF NORMALCY. WE FEEL CONFIDENT AND DARE TO BELIEVE IN A BRIGHTER FUTURE WITH HOPE IN OUR HEARTS.

ANCHORED IN HOPE IS AN ANTHOLOGY OF TWENTY-SIX SHORT REFLECTIONS, ONE FOR EACH LETTER OF THE ALPHABET. EACH REFLECTION ADDRESSES A MEANINGFUL THEME, OFFERING GUIDANCE TO ENHANCE YOUR *QUALITY OF LIFE*. THE

REFLECTIONS CONTAIN PEARLS OF WISDOM TO TOUCH YOUR HEART AND EMPOWER YOU TO LIVE YOUR MOST AMAZING LIFE THROUGHOUT ALL ITS SEASONS. THE JOURNALING PAGES ARE FOR YOU TO JOT DOWN WHAT YOUR HEART SPEAKS TO YOU. TAKE THE TIME TO REFLECT ON YOUR FEELINGS IN RESPONSE TO THE REFLECTIONS. I HOPE YOU CAN EMBRACE THE MOMENT. FOCUS ON BEING AWARE OF ALL THAT IS HAPPENING NOW. AND BE MINDFUL OF THE MOMENTS CLUSTERED TOGETHER TO SHAPE THE ATMOSPHERE AND TEMPERAMENT OF YOUR DAY.

OUR LIVES HAVE CHANGED DUE TO THE CHALLENGES WE HAVE LIVED THROUGH DURING THE PAST FEW YEARS. LIFE WILL NEVER BE QUITE THE SAME. ONLY MORE PROFOUND BECAUSE OF THE SHARED EXPERIENCES THAT BONDED US TOGETHER. HELPING US FIND LIGHT IN THE SHADES OF DARKNESS. WE HAVE FINE-TUNED OUR EMPATHIC NATURE TO SEE OTHERS DIFFERENTLY AND TO LOVE MORE TENDERLY.

IN OUR NOISY WORLD. IT BEHOOVES US TO CULTIVATE QUIET. FOR ME. A QUIET WALK ON THE BEACH RENEWS MY SPIRIT. I REMIND MYSELF TO BREATHE. SLOW DOWN. PUT ASIDE WORRIES. AND LISTEN TO THE SOUNDS OF SILENCE ECHOING WITH THE RHYME OF THE SPLASHING WAVES. BEACHES ARE PEACEFUL PLACES. VOID OF THE NOISE OF THE HUSTLE AND BUSTLE OF OUR CHAOTIC WORLD. STAMPING FOOTPRINTS IN THE SAND AND WATCHING THE OCEAN SURF ERASE THEM HELPS ME APPRECIATE THE SACREDNESS OF THE PRESENT MOMENT. LIKE THE DISAPPEARING FOOTPRINTS ON THE BEACH. OUR LIVES ARE BUT A FLEETING IMPRINT ON THIS WORLD. BREATHE SLOWLY. TAKE A DEEP BREATH...BREATHE.

An Alphabetical Anthology

Aging with Grace:
The Gift and the Struggle

We may fear getting older, but many blessings grace us as we slow down and enjoy the evening years of our lives. Aging is an extraordinary process that allows us to become a better version of our authentic selves. It doesn't have to be a barrier to a fulfilling and happy life. We cannot control some things in life, and aging's physical diminishment is among them. If we have the good fortune to grow old, we get to celebrate the journey into our tranquil and noble years. Not everyone has that privilege. Looking in the mirror may reveal physical changes: a more fragile appearance with wrinkles, graying hair, and maybe even a shorter stature. Beneath that appearance, there is a person with a determined resilience. As survivors of many life experiences, we make every effort to accept and adapt to our physical limitations and quietly cope with our aches and pains. With the blessing of years, we recognize

OUR MISTAKES AND SHORTCOMINGS. WE ARE TALENTED AT IMPROVISING, AND OUR CREATIVITY FAR SURPASSES OUR LIMITATIONS. GUIDED BY A SPIRITUAL QUEST, WE RELY ON OUR FAITH TO FIND SERENITY AND PEACE.

FRIENDSHIPS ARE ONE OF OUR GREATEST ASSETS IN THE EVENING OF OUR LIVES. AS WE LIVE INTO OUR SENIOR YEARS, WE HAVE THE TIME TO ENJOY REMINISCING WITH FRIENDS WHO SHARE SIMILAR LIFE EXPERIENCES. NO MATTER HOW DIFFICULT THE HARDSHIPS OF OUR YOUTH, IT IS HEARTENING TO SHARE THE FOND MEMORIES OF THE "GOOD OLD DAYS."

THE OLDER YEARS ANNOUNCE THE NEED FOR AN EXTRA PUSH GETTING OUT OF A CHAIR, CAUTION ON THE STAIRS, KNOWING IT IS OFFICIALLY TIME TO STAY OFF LADDERS AND SAY NO TO HIGH HEELS. WITH AGE COMES THE MOURNING OF LOVED ONES WHO HAVE GONE BEFORE US. OUR HEARTS ACHE AS WE REGROUP TO CELEBRATE AND CHERISH THEIR MEMORIES. COUNTING OUR BLESSINGS BECOMES OUR FOCUS. AS WE LEARN THE ART OF LETTING GO, WE DISCOVER LESS IS MORE, AND LIFE IS A PRECIOUS COMMODITY. THIS EARTHLY JOURNEY HAS AN END, BUT THE WISDOM OF YEARS TELLS US TO STAY PRESENT AND CELEBRATE TODAY'S BLESSINGS. OUR TOMORROWS ARE IN GOD'S HANDS.

AMONG THE STRUGGLES OF AGING GRACEFULLY IS MEMORY LOSS. FORGETFULNESS AND OTHER PHYSICAL LIMITATIONS CAUSE SIDE EFFECTS. IT IS NOT UNCOMMON FOR THE ELDERLY TO EXPERIENCE BRAIN FOG, LOWER ENERGY, AND WORRY ABOUT THE FUTURE. PHYSICAL EXERCISE AT ANY AGE IS A POSITIVE APPROACH TO HOLISTIC HEALTH. WE SEEK THE ENERGY TO KEEP GOING AND STRIVE TO BE AS ACTIVE AS POSSIBLE. THE GIFT OF LIVING AND DOING ACCORDING TO OUR BODY'S INTERNAL

> **"**
> WHEN GRACE IS JOINED
> WITH WRINKLES IT IS
> ADORABLE.
> THERE IS AN
> UNSPEAKABLE DAWN
> IN HAPPY OLD AGE.
> *Victor Hugo*
> **"**

SENSORS IS THE MOST REMARKABLE GRACE. IT IS ESSENTIAL TO TAKE GENTLE CARE OF OURSELVES AND SEEK BALANCE WITH MODERATION. AGING WITH GRACE IS NOT FOR THE FAINT-HEARTED. ACCEPTING THE SLOWING DOWN PROCESS IS NOT EASY. THE MOST GRACIOUS AMONG US STRIVE TO BE PEACEMAKERS, LIVING IN THE PRESENT WITH

A GRATEFUL HEART. AMAZINGLY, WE ADAPT WELL TO THE EFFECTS OF AGING, ALWAYS FINDING A GOOD REASON TO CELEBRATE THE GIFT OF LIFE.

WITH THE GIFT OF TIME, GIVING BACK SEEMS RIGHT AND VERY REWARDING. WE PRAY FOR THE GRACE TO SEE MORE CLEARLY AND LOVE MORE TENDERLY. THE AGING PROCESS HAS TAUGHT US TO STAY CALM DURING A CRISIS AND TO UNDERSTAND RATHER THAN JUDGE. ON A POSITIVE NOTE, WE NOW HAVE THE TIME TO DO THE THINGS WE HAVE PUT OFF FOR YEARS: READ BOOKS, GO TO MOVIES, HAVE A LEISURELY LUNCH WITH A FRIEND, AND CHECK OUR BUCKET LIST AND SAY, "WHY NOT?" OUR MATURE PERSPECTIVE REMINDS US THAT THE DAYS OF IMPRESSING OTHERS ARE OVER. TITLES, ACCOMPLISHMENTS, AND DEGREES DO NOT DEFINE US. WE STRIVE TO LIVE BY GRACE, NOT BY PERFECTION. IT IS A JOY TO TAKE THE TIME TO SMELL THE FLOWERS AND EMBRACE ALL WE ARE AS WE CONTINUE TO GROW IN WISDOM, AGE, AND GRACE. ENJOY THE BLESSINGS OF THIS DAY!

PONDER THIS THOUGHT: "THE AFTERNOON KNOWS WHAT THE MORNING NEVER SUSPECTED."

Robert Frost

We all have different paths in life.
As in purpose, so is happiness.
As our purposes differ,
so do our roads to happiness differ,
through we may have common grounds.

Ogwo David Emenke

DATE _____

LET YOUR HEART SPEAK

JOURNALING . . .

Being YOU is Enough

It's easy for us to compare ourselves to others and perceive them as better than you. Often, what we observe in others usually does not reveal their complexities. It is common to have a public persona that screens out the private matters of our hearts and gives the message that all is well. No matter how we feel or what burdens we carry, we shield others from knowing our struggles. In subtle ways, we have become masters at the art of hiding behind an invisible mask to conceal our feelings, playing the game of pretending. Unlike wearing a protective covering to limit the spread of COVID-19, our invisible mask protects us from revealing the hurts that weigh heavy on

> You may not control all the events that happen to you. But you can decide not to be reduced by them.
>
> *Maya Angelou*

OUR HEARTS. WE WORK HARD AT PROJECTING A POSITIVE IMAGE. BELIEVING WE ARE NOT QUITE GOOD ENOUGH. THE BELIEF WE ARE LESS THAN IS EMBEDDED IN OUR PSYCHE AND DIFFICULT TO ERASE. UNDERSTANDING THE SOURCE OF OUR SELF-DOUBTS HELPS US LET GO OF OUR EMOTIONAL PAIN. WE ALL HAVE A FUNDAMENTAL NEED TO LOVE AND TO BE LOVED. IT IS A UNIVERSAL LONGING. WE DO NOT WANT TO DISAPPOINT BECAUSE BEING REJECTED IS SO PAINFUL. SLOWLY. WAKE UP THE TRUE YOU UNDERNEATH THE PRETENSE AND CAMOUFLAGE. IT IS A WELCOMED RELIEF TO FEEL SAFE ENOUGH TO REMOVE THE INVISIBLE MASK. EMBRACE THE PERSON YOU HAVE COME TO KNOW AND UNDERSTAND, THE PERSON WITH STRENGTHS AND WEAKNESSES. BELIEVE IN YOUR GOODNESS. YOUR UNIQUENESS. AND YOUR UNIQUE QUALITIES. AVOID NEGATIVE SELF-TALK AND COMPARING YOURSELF WITH OTHERS. YOUR HAPPINESS INCREASES AS YOU EXPLORE THE MANY FACETS OF YOURSELF THAT AFFIRM YOUR AUTHENTICITY. LOVE AND HONOR THE EXPERIENCES THAT SHAPED YOU. DON'T LET THE NEGATIVE COMMENTS AND UGLINESS IN OTHERS DEGRADE THE BEAUTY WITHIN YOU. YOU COUNT! YOU ARE A GIFT TO OUR WORLD. BE YOU. THE WORLD WILL ADJUST. GROW THROUGH WHAT YOU ARE GOING THROUGH AND KNOW EVERY NEW DAY OFFERS YOU THE CHANCE TO REWRITE YOUR STORY. STRIVE TO MAKE CHOICES THAT AFFIRM YOUR GOODNESS AND ADDRESS YOUR INSECURITIES. ONCE YOU COME TO APPRECIATE WHO YOU ARE. YOU WILL BEGIN LIVING IN PEACEFUL HARMONY.

YOU MAY BE FRUSTRATED WITH YOUR LIMITATIONS. FAULTS. AND CIRCUMSTANCES. SOME BEYOND YOUR CONTROL. WHAT YOU THINK YOU NEED AND WANT MAY NOT BE WHAT WILL BRING YOU HAPPINESS. HAPPINESS IS FINDING CONTENTMENT WITH WHO YOU ARE. WHAT MAKES YOU A BLESSING TO OTHERS? WHAT ARE THE QUALITIES THAT MAKE YOU SPECIAL? BEING YOU IS ENOUGH BUT NOT AN EXCUSE TO STOP BECOMING. EVERY DAY IS A NEW BEGINNING AND A NEW OPPORTUNITY TO PARTICIPATE IN THE ART OF BECOMING. YOUR LIVED EXPERIENCES MOLD YOUR OUTLOOK. CHALLENGING YOU TO EXPAND YOUR HORIZON AND CHASE AFTER YOUR DREAMS. THERE IS NO NEED TO EXPLAIN YOURSELF. YOU OWE NO ONE AN EXPLANATION. YOUR LIFE IS YOURS. NOT THEIRS.

HUMBLY ACCEPT THE COMPLIMENTS THAT COME YOUR WAY. THEY ARE A TRUE REFLECTION OF YOUR AUTHENTIC SELF. YOUR PEERS ARE YOUR BEST AND MOST HONEST CRITICS. START EACH DAY BY BEING TRUE TO YOURSELF. TAKE OFF THE MASK

YOU HAVE BEEN HIDING BEHIND AND EXPOSE THE REAL YOU, WITH ALL YOUR FLAWS AND IMPERFECTIONS. MORE IMPORTANTLY, BELIEVE IN YOUR GOODNESS. ACCEPT OTHERS THE WAY YOU WISH TO BE ACCEPTED. DON'T JUDGE OR REJECT THEM BASED ON WHAT YOU PERCEIVE TO BE THEIR LIMITATIONS; INSTEAD, TAKE THE TIME TO FIND THEIR UNIQUE QUALITIES. ABOVE ALL ELSE, STRIVE TO FIND YOUR INNER PEACE.

STEVE JOBS REMINDS US, *"OUR TIME IS LIMITED. SO, DON'T WASTE IT LIVING SOMEONE ELSE'S LIFE."* INSTEAD, EMBRACE WHO YOU ARE AND PRAY FOR THE COURAGE TO LET GO OF WHO YOU ARE NOT. HAPPINESS IS NOT ALWAYS ABOUT HAVING THE VERY BEST. IT IS ABOUT MAKING THE BEST OF EVERYTHING AND EVERY SITUATION. SO, WHEN EVERYTHING IS CRASHING DOWN AROUND YOU, BREATHE AND TAKE CARE OF THE MOST IMPORTANT PART OF YOUR WORLD, YOU. AND, WHEN LIFE SHINES AN ABUNDANCE OF LIGHT ON YOU, HELP LIGHT THE PATH OF THOSE WALKING IN DENSE FOG. AS MAYA ANGELOU CHALLENGES US, *"TRY TO BE THE RAINBOW IN SOMEONE ELSE'S CLOUD."* WE JOURNEY TOGETHER, AND TOGETHER, WE LIFT UP EACH OTHER. AND AS YOU UPLIFT OTHERS, REMEMBER TO BE GOOD TO YOURSELF.

PONDER THIS THOUGHT: *"BE YOURSELF; EVERYONE ELSE IS ALREADY TAKEN."*

Oscar Wilde

JUST IN CASE ... NO ONE

TOLD YOU TODAY...

DATE _____

LET YOUR HEART SPEAK

JOURNALING . . .

You are the gift
our world is waiting for.

The time is now

to share your uniqueness

as a gift and a blessing.

DO YOU HAVE THE

courage

TO BRING FORTH THE

treasures

THAT ARE HIDDEN

within you?

Elizabeth Gilbert

COURAGE TO RISK & TAKE CHANCES

S COTT PECK REMINDS US, *"LIFE IS DIFFICULT."* IN HIS BOOK, *"THE ROAD LESS TRAVELED,"* HE SHARES THAT LIFE'S CHALLENGES CAN EITHER MAKE OR BREAK US. IT TAKES COURAGE TO LIVE IN THE SHADES OF DIFFICULT TIMES, NOT KNOWING HOW LONG THEY WILL LAST OR WHAT THE OUTCOMES WILL BE. THE MANY UNKNOWNS ARE WHAT PARALYZE US FROM FEELING HOPEFUL. AT THE DAY'S END, WE ARE OFTEN SURPRISED BY THE UNEXPECTED HAPPENINGS THAT CREPT INTO OUR TWENTY-FOUR-HOUR DAY. WE STEP UP TO THE PLATE WITH AMAZEMENT AND COURAGE AND RESPOND APPROPRIATELY.

THE WORD "COURAGE" HAS ROOTS IN OLD FRENCH COEUR *("HEART"),* FROM THE LATIN WORD FOR HEART, COR. HAVING COURAGE MEANS MOVING FROM THE HEART TO DO WHAT IS RIGHT, DESPITE FEAR OR POTENTIAL DANGER. OUR SOUL KNOWS THE TRUTH AND WHAT WE NEED TO DO TO ACT JUSTLY AND TO LOVE TENDERLY.

As survivors of many near catastrophes, we can put up with almost anything, at least for a while. It takes courage to stay positive during a trying time. Living through challenging situations can build character, teach patience, and broaden our priorities. Taking it a day, even a minute at a time, helps prioritize things and cope with disappointments and losses. Living through challenging times takes courage and confirms the belief that we can survive and even thrive as we discover the depth of our resilience.

A few years after I survived advanced-stage ovarian cancer, I was restless and confused. I didn't know how I wanted to spend the rest of my life. I was floundering and searching for what, I was not sure. At the medical center where I received my chemotherapy and had my surgeries, a staff nurse told me about an Outward Bound program in Colorado for cancer survivors. A few weeks later, I was on a plane to Colorado to risk and stretch my limits with the hope of discovering a new horizon. I was in uncharted territory with no idea of what was about to take place. It took courage to show up a thousand miles from home, in a strange place, to spend time with cancer survivors that I had never met. During the flight, I questioned why I was opting to risk again after taking so many risks. I realized I was on a quest to understand myself. It was humbling and empowering, and the reward of risking filled me with new hope. Until tested, we never know the depth of our resilience.

> "Courage doesn't always roar. Sometimes courage is a quiet voice. At the end of the day saying I will try again tomorrow.
> Mary Anne Radmacher"

It is to your advantage to find comfort in your vulnerability and fear of risk-taking. It is rewarding to be decisive about your goals and chart a course to attain them. What is the challenge worth to you? There is no guarantee what you are undertaking will be successful. You may fail and discover you are not in control of many things. However, when the risk

PAYS OFF AND YOU ACCOMPLISH YOUR GOAL, YOU BECOME MORE RESILIENT AND CONFIDENT. ALTHOUGH IT CAN BE SCARY, IT IS ALSO EXCITING. FAITH AND HOPE GO TOGETHER. RISK USUALLY IMPLIES CHANGE. YOU RISK BECAUSE YOU ARE RESTLESS AND SEE THE NEED FOR CHANGE. CHANGE IS A FACT OF LIFE, AND CHANGE MEANS THINGS WILL BE DIFFERENT — TO WHAT EXTENT, YOU DON'T KNOW.

I DON'T BELIEVE WE ARE SEARCHING FOR A PERFECT LIFE, JUST A MORE MEANINGFUL ONE WHERE THE ORDINARY GREETS THE EXTRAORDINARY, AND WE REJOICE WITH SURPRISE. IN ALL THINGS, STRIVE TO SEEK THE TRUTH OF WHO YOU ARE. YOU ARE COURAGEOUS AND WILL RISE TO DO THE UNBELIEVABLE WHEN NECESSARY. REMEMBER, YOU ARE CAPABLE OF AMAZING THINGS.

PONDER THIS THOUGHT: *"EVERY ADVERSITY BRINGS NEW EXPERIENCES AND NEW LESSONS."*

Lailah Gift Akita

"Don't be afraid of your fears.
They're not there to scare you.
They're there to let you know
that something is worth it."

C. JoyBell C.

DATE _____

LET YOUR HEART SPEAK

JOURNALING . . .

DARE TO DREAM

ABINGTON

GOODWIN

DARE TO DREAM

W HEN YOU DARE TO DREAM AND BELIEVE IN YOURSELF, YOU WILL BE SURPRISED AS YOU SURPASS YOUR EXPECTATIONS. DON'T BE AFRAID TO REACH FOR THE STARS.

DEAL WITH YOUR DEEPEST FEARS. OFTEN, THE FEELING OF INADEQUACY IS THE FEAR THAT CRIPPLES AND PREVENTS YOU FROM SUCCEEDING. WITH GOD'S GRACE AND THE SUPPORT OF OTHERS, YOU HAVE ALL IT TAKES TO DARE AND TO BELIEVE IN YOURSELF AND YOUR DREAMS. DARING INVOLVES STEPPING OUT OF YOUR COMFORT ZONE AND COMMITTING TO HARD WORK.

> " THIS WORLD IS
> VAST ENOUGH
> TO HANDLE ANYTHING
> YOU DARE
> TO DREAM.
> *Hill Harper* "

HAVE YOU EVER BEEN TOLD YOU HAVE A GIFT, A SPECIAL TALENT, A PERSONALITY THAT IS WARM AND CHARMING, MAKING OTHERS FEEL COMFORTABLE?

Believe what those close to you tell you. They have a good insight into your talents and abilities. You need to believe and dare to risk to reach your goal. Doubting your abilities is a huge block to success. Begin the hard work of accomplishing your goal. Remember, it is a huge commitment, and the road will not be easy. Failures, frustrations, disappointments, and roadblocks will cause you to doubt, but give it time. Sometimes it is easier to give up instead of accepting the challenge and giving it your all. Let go of your doubt and trust in your God-given talents. Commit to DARE to DREAM and take the first step to have your dream come true. It is never too late to begin a new adventure. Don't let age be your disqualifier. Regardless of age, if you can dream it, most of the time, you can achieve it. Unearth your dreams of years ago and pursue them. You now have the time.

Another aspect of dreaming is daring to empower yourself and others by speaking up without fearing rejection or ridicule. When you dare to believe in yourself by lifting your voice, you are on your way to becoming a better version of yourself. You never know what your testimony does to inspire others. You never know who you are helping by having the courage to speak your truth. Silence is not the answer. Marianne Williamson reminds us, *"As we let our light shine, we unconsciously permit other people to do the same. As we are liberated from our fear, our presence liberates others."* Your resilience will steer you in the right direction. Dare to believe in yourself because others are waiting for permission from you to let their light shine.

As you walk into the future, have courage and believe your future holds endless possibilities. Try to overcome the fear and self-doubt and work toward building your self-confidence and self-esteem. Believe you are talented and use your gifts for the good of yourself and others. Be proactive in achieving your goal. It takes hard work and commitment to stay enthusiastic and focused. Hold on to the expectation that what you want will happen, and daily commit to it.

BELIEVE IN YOURSELF BECAUSE NOT WALKING IN YOUR PURPOSE IS TOO GREAT A MISTAKE FOR YOU TO MAKE. THE LITTLE BOY IN THE PICTURE HAS BIG DREAMS OF BECOMING A FIREFIGHTER. HE DRESSES THE PART AND ROLE-PLAYS IN HIS DREAMS. CHILDREN DREAM DREAMS. AND GROWNUPS BELIEVE THEIR CHILDHOOD DREAMS WILL COME TRUE.

KEEP GOING EVEN WHEN THE GOING GETS TOUGH. FOCUS ON YOUR GOAL TO ACCOMPLISH YOUR DREAMS AND GIVE IT YOUR VERY BEST. SUCCESS DOESN'T HAPPEN OVERNIGHT. SOMETIMES IT TAKES YEARS OF TRYING. THE JOURNEY TO THE DESTINATION IS AT LEAST AS IMPORTANT AS THE DESTINATION ITSELF. YOUR LIFE'S JOURNEY IS ABOUT LIVING EVERY DAY WITH A SENSE OF MEANING AND CONTENTMENT. TRY TO LIVE IN THE PRESENT AND CELEBRATE THE LITTLE MILESTONES ALONG YOUR WAY.

PONDER THIS THOUGHT: *"PATIENCE IS NOT PASSIVE WAITING. PATIENCE IS ACTIVE ACCEPTANCE OF THE PROCESS REQUIRED TO ATTAIN YOUR GOALS AND DREAMS."*

Ray A. Davis

Dare
to
Believe
Dream
Live

DATE: _____

LET YOUR HEART SPEAK

JOURNALING . . .

EMPATHY
FELT AND EXPRESSED

LEARNING TO STAND IN SOMEBODY ELSE'S SHOES, TO SEE THROUGH THEIR EYES, IS HOW A BOND OF TRUST DEVELOPS. PEOPLE NOTICE HOW MUCH YOU CARE MORE THAN HOW MUCH YOU KNOW. LEO BUSCAGLIA SHARES A GOOD INSIGHT. *"TOO OFTEN, WE UNDERESTIMATE THE POWER OF A TOUCH, A SMILE, A KIND WORD, A LISTENING EAR, AN HONEST COMPLIMENT, OR THE SMALLEST ACT OF CARING."* EMPATHY IS THE ABILITY TO IMAGINE WHAT SOMEONE ELSE IS FEELING OR WHAT IT'S LIKE TO BE IN THEIR SITUATION. EMPATHY IS A QUALITY THAT ALLOWS US TO FEEL THE HURT OR PAIN OF ANOTHER AS IF IT WERE OUR PAIN. BEING EMPATHIC IS A WAY OF BEING ONE WITH ANOTHER IN THEIR PAIN.

IF YOU HAVE A GOOD INSIGHT INTO THE FEELINGS ANOTHER IS EXPERIENCING, YOU CAN UNDERSTAND THEIR EMOTIONS AND STRUGGLES AS IF THEY WERE YOUR OWN.

You know, and you take notice. No experiencing. Being empathic is also being compassionate. If you

are compassionate and empathic, you are a gift when someone needs to be understood and loved. So many people seem fine on the exterior but carry heavy emotional burdens and feel deep anguish inside. The empathic person can see beneath the surface and resonate with another's emotional pain.

Your emotional challenges empower you with an understanding to respond empathically to the struggles of others. Going through a difficult time can deplete your energy and cause you to feel depressed and overwhelmed. Try to focus on good coping skills, seek out friends and professional help to guide you to transcend the hurt and process the heartache. Your life will be richer, and you will be more sensitive to the pain of others because of your journey through challenging times.

Your empathic nature is a source of healing to others. It is a special gift to be able to listen empathically without judgment. Your hurting friends need someone to understand their pain and be with them in the rawness of their agony. They do not want you to solve their problem but need you to be emotionally supportive during the darkness of their struggle. They need the assurance that you care and that better days are ahead. An understanding friend can be a lifesaver in troubled times. Don't shy away when your friend is brokenhearted. Reach out with loving kindness, let your friend know you care, and you will not abandon him during a struggling time.

Qualities of an empathic person include being vulnerable and listening intensely to the spoken words and, more importantly, to the unspoken words. Avoid making assumptions and withhold judgments. Instead, show you deeply care by your gentle and prayerful presence. In a time of need, an empathetic person can save a life.

Empathy is tender-heartedness felt and expressed. To be empathic is to look into another's eyes and know that what you see in the hurting person is only bruised but not broken. Understanding the role of

WHOLENESS, WELLNESS, AND HEALING CAN HELP MEND THEIR HURT AND ANXIOUS FEELINGS.

Empathy strengthens our resolve to reach out to strangers when they are in crisis. Former President Barack Obama said, "The biggest deficit that we have in our society and in the world right now is an empathy deficit. We are in great need of people being able to stand in somebody else's shoes and see the world through their eyes." What do you do to help fill the empathy deficit in our wounded society?

Ponder this thought: "First of all, if you learn a simple trick, Scout, you'll get along a lot better with all kinds of folks. You never really understand a person until you consider things from his point of view . . . until you climb into his skin and walk around in it."

Atticus, "To Kill A Mockingbird"

I THINK WE ALL HAVE EMPATHY.
WE MAY NOT HAVE ENOUGH
COURAGE TO DISPLAY IT.

Maya Angelou

DATE _____

LET YOUR HEART SPEAK

JOURNALING . . .

FRIENDSHIP

a precious

gift.

Friendship: A Precious Gift

To have a good friend for a lifetime is a gift to celebrate. A special friend shares a bond with you that is a blessing beyond measure. Time and distance do not diminish the bond that seals your friendship. As the song reminds us: *People who need people are the luckiest people in the world.* In many ways, it is a mystery that draws two people to each other as special friends. Friendship is a relationship of mutual affection.

A special friend knows you inside and out, knows what you love and fear, your deepest secrets, pains, mistakes, failures, and dreams. You feel safe knowing your friend has your best interests at heart. In the presence of

> " Friendship is born at that moment when one person says to another: What! You too? I thought I was the only one.
>
> *C.S. Lewis*
> "

YOUR FRIEND, YOU CAN BE YOURSELF. YOU DO NOT HAVE TO PRETEND YOU ARE OKAY WHEN YOU ARE NOT. A FRIEND IS THERE TO CELEBRATE YOUR GOOD NEWS, REJOICES WITH YOU WHEN YOU ARE HAPPY, AND IS BY YOUR SIDE WHEN YOU ARE HURTING OR SAD. THERE ARE NO LIMITATIONS TO HOW A FRIEND WILL SUPPORT YOU. A FRIEND WILL PRAY FOR YOU AND WITH YOU, KNOWING WHEN TO TALK AND WHEN TO BE SILENT. A DEAR FRIEND IS ALWAYS HONEST WITH YOU, DOES NOT MINCE WORDS, AND ALWAYS HAS YOUR BACK, HELPING YOU SHINE IN YOUR BEST LIGHT. A FRIEND SHOWS RESPECT, HONORS YOUR UNIQUENESS, AND TOLERATES YOUR IDIOSYNCRASIES.

WHEN YOU FEEL LOST AND SCARED, YOUR FRIEND IS THERE AS A SOUNDING BOARD, NOT JUDGING BUT UNDERSTANDING. WHEN YOU NEED SOMEONE WHO CARES, YOUR FRIEND IS THERE. WHEN ALL IS RIGHT WITH YOUR WORLD, YOUR FRIEND SHARES YOUR PEACEFULNESS. YOUR FRIEND IS YOUR CONFIDANT, THE PERSON WHO LOVES YOU UNCONDITIONALLY AND STANDS BY YOU THROUGH THICK AND THIN. A TRUE FRIEND CHALLENGES YOU TO BE A BETTER PERSON. THE BEAUTY OF A SHARED FRIENDSHIP IS ITS RECIPROCITY. BEING A SPECIAL FRIEND MEANS YOU ARE COMPASSIONATE AND CARING. A FRIEND STANDS BY YOU EVEN WHEN OTHERS DOUBT YOU AND IS NOT WORRIED ABOUT LOSING POPULARITY BECAUSE OF YOU. THAT FRIEND WILL DROP EVERYTHING TO BE BY YOUR SIDE.

YOUR FRIEND HAS THE UNCANNY ABILITY TO READ YOUR MIND BEFORE YOU SPEAK, JUST BY EXCHANGING A GLANCE, YOU KNOW PRECISELY WHAT THE OTHER IS THINKING. A FRIEND DOES NOT BETRAY YOUR CONFIDENCE, DOES NOT JUDGE YOU, BUT UNDERSTANDS "WHY" EVEN BEFORE YOU KNOW "WHY." YOUR FRIEND CHEERS YOU ON AND STANDS BY YOUR SIDE WHEN YOU STRUGGLE, AND CELEBRATES WITH YOU IN GOOD TIMES. A FRIEND DOES NOT TRY TO OUTDO YOU, DOES NOT ACT SUPERIOR. THERE IS NO COMPETITION; RATHER, GRATITUDE FOR SHARED EXPERIENCES. A FRIEND GIVES WITHOUT EXPECTING ANYTHING IN RETURN. WE HAVE MANY ACQUAINTANCES IN LIFE, BUT A LOYAL FRIEND IS A TREASURE TO CHERISH.

GOD PUTS FRIENDS IN OUR LIVES AT THE RIGHT TIME TO GUIDE US ON OUR JOURNEYS. THEY HELP US FIND OUR RHYTHM AND LIGHTEN OUR STEPS. VALUED AND LOVED AND MUCH APPRECIATED, SOMETIMES THEY ARE MEANT TO JOURNEY WITH US FOR JUST A WHILE AND THEN PART, LEAVING AN IMPRINT ON OUR HEARTS FOREVER.

It is a special blessing when two childhood friends can continue to share their friendship into adulthood and senior years. It is a joy for old friends to reminisce about the precious memories of their past, laugh about the silly times, close calls, failed romances, crazy incidents that were so important at the time.

The poem by Samantha Glovier describes the blessing of being a true friend. "A true friend is someone who will always be there when a friend is in need. A true friend will see the things you see and never disrespect you for what you believe." Friendship is a precious gift.

Ponder this thought: "Friendship is always a sweet responsibility, never an opportunity."

Khalil Gibran

DATE _____

LET YOUR HEART SPEAK

JOURNALING . . .

The pain
of an
aching heart

GRIEF:

THE PAIN OF AN ACHING HEART

GOING THROUGH A DIFFICULT LOSS: THE DEATH OF A LOVED ONE. A BREAKUP. A DIVORCE. THE LOSS OF A JOB - IS DEVASTATING. EACH KIND OF LOSS HAS ITS HEARTACHE THAT CAN CRIPPLE YOU EMOTIONALLY. YES. LIFE IS COMPLICATED. AND GRIEVING A LOSS IS EMOTIONALLY TAXING. SOME LOSSES ARE MORE COMPLICATED THAN OTHERS. IT IS A PAINFUL REALITY THAT MAKES YOU

> " GRIEF NEVER ENDS BUT IT CHANGES US. IT IS A PASSAGE, NOT A PLACE TO STAY. GRIEF IS NOT A SIGN OF WEAKNESS.. NOR A LACK OF FAITH. IT IS THE PRICE OF LOVE.
>
> *Anonymous* "

QUESTION "WHY." SOMETIMES YOU DO NOT KNOW WHERE TO TURN TO FIND SOLACE, TO SEEK HEALING. NO INSURANCE POLICY CAN PROTECT YOU FROM GETTING SICK OR SUFFERING A BROKEN HEART. IT MAY PROVIDE THE CARE YOU NEED WHEN ILL AND HELP PAY FOR PSYCHOTHERAPY WHEN YOUR HEART ACHES, BUT IT PROVIDES NO IMMUNITY. WHERE DO YOU BEGIN TO FIND HOPE?

IF YOU FEEL SAD, DEPRESSED, OR ANXIOUS BECAUSE OF A LOSS, PLEASE KNOW THAT THESE ARE PAINFUL AND REAL SYMPTOMS OF GRIEVING. IT TAKES TIME TO RECOVER FROM ANY LOSS. A SIGNIFICANT LOSS CAN SEEM IMPOSSIBLE TO RECOVER FROM WHEN THE TUGS AT YOUR HEARTSTRINGS ARE SO POWERFUL. YET, AS UNBELIEVABLE AS IT MAY SEEM, THE HUMAN SPIRIT IS RESILIENT. THE GRIEVING PROCESS TAKES TIME, AND THAT TIMELINE IS UNIQUE TO EACH PERSON AND EVERY SITUATION. A COLLEAGUE AND FRIEND, PAUL TSCHUDI, REFERS TO LOSS AS A LIFE TRANSITION. *IN ORDER TO HAVE A NEW BEGINNING, YOU HAVE TO LET GO OF SOMETHING...IT IS ABOUT LETTING GO OF THAT WHICH WAS AND PREPARING FOR THAT WHICH IS TO COME – A NORMAL AND NATURAL PART OF LIFE. PERHAPS IT MAKES US MORE FULLY HUMAN.* TO MOURN A LOSS IS A WAY TO EASE THE GRIEF THAT GRIPS YOUR ENTIRE BEING. MOURNING IS AN ESSENTIAL STEP IN PROCESSING YOUR LOSS. WHILE THE PAIN LESSENS OVER TIME, COPING WITH ALL THE SYMPTOMS IS A LIFETIME TASK. SOMETIMES THE LOSS SEEMS VERY UNREAL. AT TIMES IT FEELS VERY DISTANT, AND AT OTHER TIMES IT FEELS LIKE YESTERDAY. YOUR MEMORIES ARE REMINDERS OF WHAT ONCE WAS. AS YOU GRIEVE, YOU MAY FIND YOURSELF AVOIDING FRIENDS AND SOCIAL ENGAGEMENTS. REMEMBER: THERE IS NO RIGHT OR WRONG WAY TO GRIEVE. YOUR WAY IS THE RIGHT WAY FOR YOU. LET YOUR HEART LEAD YOU AS YOU LIVE THROUGH THE RAWNESS OF YOUR LOSS. C. S. LEWIS SHARES, *GRIEF IS LIKE A LONG VALLEY, A WINDING VALLEY WHERE ANY BEND MAY REVEAL A TOTALLY NEW LANDSCAPE.* YOU CANNOT PREDICT WHAT YOU WILL EXPERIENCE AS YOU WORK THROUGH THE EMOTIONAL UPS AND DOWNS THAT ARE NORMAL DURING THE GRIEVING PROCESS.

AS A SOCIETY, WE FIND WAYS TO DENY THE FINALITY OF DEATH. WE HAVE ADOPTED THE WORD "PASSED" TO REPLACE THE WORD "DIED." AS DIFFICULT AS IT IS, WE NEED TO FIND A WAY TO GRADUALLY PROCESS THE LOSS SO WE CAN ACCEPT THE REALITY THAT OUR LOVED ONE HAS DIED. IT IS A BIG STEP TOWARD FINDING PEACE.

There are degrees of loss, and situations cause multiple losses, some happening simultaneously. Living through loss while struggling to make sense of it is challenging. While grieving, it is important to take gentle care, lower expectations, and give ourselves the time to do the things we need to do. It is okay not to be okay. There are no rules. Although your pain is very raw at first, one day, you will wake up to a better day. Until then, be good to yourself.

After a significant loss, it is possible to experience a broken heart and feel the physical and emotional pain of *"broken heart syndrome"* that can mimic heart attack symptoms. The immeasurable and devastating blow of grief is complicated and shakes us to our core. Mending a broken heart is a lengthy process. Finding the path to healing is finding a way from brokenness to wholeness. Memories once painful help fashion the potential for tomorrow's peace and contentment.

Ponder this thought: "They whom we love and lose are no longer where they were before. They are now wherever we are".

St. John Chrysostom

Lord,

Heal my aching heart.

Help me to find peace

living with the memories.

That is all I have.

Amen.

DATE _____

LET YOUR HEART SPEAK

JOURNALING . . .

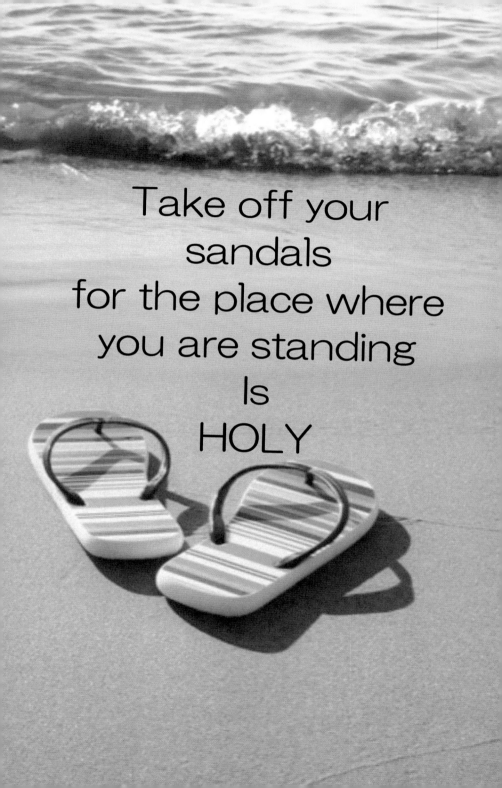

HOLY GROUND:
WHAT WE RENDER SACRED

WHAT DO YOU RENDER SACRED? WHERE IS YOUR HOLY GROUND? WHEN YOU STAND ON HOLY GROUND, YOU ARE AT A SACRED PLACE THAT TRANSCENDS YOUR FEARS AND HELPS YOU FEEL PEACEFUL AND LESS ANXIOUS. YOUR HOMES CAN BE SANCTUARIES OF HALLOWED GROUND THAT ANCHOR YOU. GOD ACCOMPANIES YOU ON YOUR DAILY JOURNEY AND WALKS WITH YOU DURING THE CHALLENGING MOMENTS OF YOUR LIFE. YOU STAND ON HOLY GROUND WHEN YOU:

- ARE ON THE SAME WAVELENGTH AS OUR SOULMATE.
- ARE ALONE BUT NOT LONELY.
- COME INTO THE PRESENCE OF GOD WHILE BEING IN THE PRESENCE OF ANOTHER.
- SEE THE GLORY OF GOD IN THE RISING AND SETTING OF THE SUN.

◆ KNOW AND FEEL THE PRESENCE OF GOD IN THE ORDINARY.

◆ REMINISCE ABOUT THE SPECIAL TIMES.

◆ FEEL THE ANGUISH OF ANOTHER AND STAY IN THEIR COMPANY TO HELP CONSOLE AND HEAL.

YES, YOU ARE LIVING ON HOLY GROUND AND GOD IS WITH YOU EVERY STEP OF THE WAY. K. J. RAMSEY OFFERS ENCOURAGEMENT: *BE GENTLE TOWARD ALL THAT REMAINS UNHEALED AND UNFINISHED IN YOU. THE SPACE BETWEEN TODAY'S HURT AND TOMORROW'S HEALING IS SACRED GROUND.* PAUSE TO RECOGNIZE THE SACRED SURROUNDING YOU. BE AN INSTRUMENT OF GOD'S LOVING PEACE AS YOU WALK THROUGH YOUR DAY. BE THE ENCOURAGING VOICE, THE QUIET SMILE, THE LOVING HEART THAT SEES THE SACRED IN THE HAPPENINGS OF YOUR DAY. AND, AS YOU CLOSE YOUR EYES AT NIGHT, THANK GOD FOR BEING ABLE TO TREAD ON HOLY GROUND AND FOR THE GIFT OF SEEING THE SACRED SURROUNDING YOU. *REMOVE THE SANDALS FROM YOUR FEET, FOR THE PLACE WHERE YOU ARE STANDING IS HOLY GROUND.* EXODUS 3:5.

AS YOU STAND IN YOUR SPACE, ON YOUR HOLY GROUND, LET GO OF THE PAST SO THE PAST CAN LET GO OF YOU. EVERY DAY IS A NEW BEGINNING. BE STILL....SLOW DOWN...TAKE A DEEP BREATH...AND CONTINUE ON. NEVER STOP BELIEVING BEAUTIFUL THINGS CAN HAPPEN, EVEN IN THE MIDST OF CHAOS.

PONDER THIS THOUGHT. *BE PATIENT WITH YOURSELF. SELF-GROWTH IS TENDER; IT'S HOLY GROUND. THERE'S NO GREATER INVESTMENT.*

 Stephen Covey

Holy Ground

Alethea Kehas

I'm not going to tell you that the moon
keeps the secrets of the tides
because you hold the ocean in your body.
When you are still, feel the waves rushing you
softly to the edges,
bringing you back to center.
You were not born broken and forgotten
You were birthed with the strength of cohesion
and the force of a division that remembers unity.

ONE THOUSAND LIVES MIGHT BRING YOU BACK
TO THE PLACE OF ORIGIN
OR YOU CAN GO THERE NOW.
RIDING THE BREATH LIKE A WAVE
TO SEED THE SACRED WITHIN YOUR BODY
BECOMING THE HOLY GROUND
FERTILE TO THE QUICKENING PULSE, RIPE WITH LOVE.
IT ROCKS WITH THE MEMORY OF HOME.

As you stand upon holy ground this day,

it is your only opportunity to be a blessing

in the lives of those you meet.

Let not this opportunity go by

or you will have squandered the blessing

for which you awoke this morning.

Be that blessing!

Date _____

LET YOUR HEART SPEAK

JOURNALING . . .

INSPIRE SOMEONE TODAY:
BE A MENTOR

TAKING THE TIME TO NOTICE A YOUNG PERSON'S POTENTIAL AND ENCOURAGING THAT GIFT CAN FOREVER CHANGE THE DIRECTION OF THEIR LIFE. IT CAN OPEN THE DOOR TO UNIMAGINED POSSIBILITIES. MENTORING IS REACHING OUT TO RECOGNIZE THE UNIQUE TALENT OF ANOTHER AND WORKING TO HELP ADVANCE THEIR ABILITY.

MENTORS ARE PEOPLE WHO CAN SUPPORT, ADVISE, AND GUIDE OTHERS. MENTORING MEANS TAKING A PARTICULAR INTEREST IN ANOTHER AND NURTURING THAT PERSON AS THEY BEGIN TO FOCUS AND COMMIT THEIR TIME AND ENERGY TO PERFECT AN INNATE TALENT. MENTORING IS A GIFT THAT EMPOWERS. IT IS A POSITIVE WAY TO GIVE BACK AND EXPERIENCE JOY IN EMPOWERING ANOTHER. IT IS REWARDING TO KNOW YOUR INTEREST AND EFFORT CHANGED ANOTHER AND INFUSED A FEELING OF HOPE THAT WAS THE INCENTIVE FOR SUCCESS.

As caring adults, we give and receive informal mentoring every day. In his book, *Shared Wisdom: The Practical Art of Giving and Receiving Mentoring*, Dr. Robert Wicks offers us the opportunity to make the most of these natural encounters. He states that a mentor is a *"beautiful part of adult life...noting not to mentor is to miss one of the most rewarding experiences available: the imparting and receiving of life's wisdom."*

What does it take to be a mentor? It takes a person who has a caring heart and a passion for affirming the goodness of others. Whether you are a mentor or a mentee, the art of mentoring establishes a special bond. The benefits of mentoring are myriad. Mentoring can be immensely rewarding for both mentor and mentee, providing many opportunities to learn, share, and gain new insights. Mentoring involves working in a trusted relationship and overcoming roadblocks encountered, including the ups and downs. Good mentors have patience, enthusiasm, and a genuine desire to walk with their mentees through uncertain times. The mentor is available when obstacles seem overwhelming, offering support and guidance. Endearing relationships are born from co-journeying through the highs and lows of mentoring. The reward comes when the mentee marks a milestone and is happy and content with their accomplishment. The greatest blessing is staying in touch and sharing the good realized by your coaching and support. A mentor's gift is seeing others flourish and make a positive contribution to society.

> 66
>
> The greatest good
> you can do
> for another
> is not just to
> share your riches
> but to reveal
> to him his own.
>
> *Benjamin Disraeli*
>
> 99

Mentoring is a beautiful way of both giving back and paying forward. Grandparents are the epitome of dedicated mentors. Their unconditional love and direction are invaluable in guiding their grandchildren. The gift

OF MENTORING DOES NOT NEED TO DIMINISH AS YOU GET OLDER. YOU ARE CONSTANTLY TRANSITIONING, EVALUATING CHOICES, AND EXPLORING EVER-CHANGING TRENDS IN YOUR LIVES. YOU CAN MENTOR SAME-AGE FRIENDS AS THEY REEVALUATE THEIR CHOICES AND OPTIONS IN THEIR SENIOR YEARS. MENTORING USUALLY FOCUSES ON SHARING YOUR GIFT OF TIME, HELPING OTHERS BYPASS PITFALLS AS THEY CHOOSE TO LIVE A MEANINGFUL LIFE. YOU WILL FEEL A SENSE OF PURPOSE WHEN YOU SHARE YOUR LESSONS LEARNED AND THE WISDOM OF YOUR YEARS. CONSIDER SHARING YOUR GIFT OF MENTORING TO INSPIRE AND MAKE A POSITIVE DIFFERENCE IN ANOTHER'S LIFE. YOUR VOLUNTEER TIME AND CARING SPIRIT WILL PROVE TO BE A BLESSING.

PONDER THIS THOUGHT: "I'VE LEARNED THAT PEOPLE WILL FORGET WHAT YOU SAID. PEOPLE WILL FORGET WHAT YOU DID, BUT PEOPLE WILL NEVER FORGET HOW YOU MADE THEM FEEL."

Maya Angelou

DATE _____

LET YOUR HEART SPEAK

JOURNALING . . .

Joy of Paying it Forward

Paying it forward is doing something kind for someone after another person did something kind for you. The joy of paying it forward is that you do something for someone you do not know, not as payback, but as a kind act, expecting nothing in return. Sometimes this creates a chain reaction, and the recipient of your kindness passes it on to another. You don't have to be rich, powerful, or influential to pay it forward. You can volunteer your time to help with the needs of the less fortunate in your community, or visit the elderly and offer to assist them with little chores. Being aware of and responding to the needs of others spreads joy and makes you an instrument of God's healing love.

> "
> We make a living by what we get.
> We make a life by what we give.
> *Winston Churchill*
> "

Doing a good deed for an unsuspecting stranger is a beautiful and selfless act. Not only will it remind the person that generosity and kindness still exist in the world, but it will also encourage the benefactor to be kind and compassionate to others. Life provides many opportunities to pay it forward. All you have to do is be attentive to the possibilities. Reach beyond your circle of family, friends, and acquaintances to consider strangers as recipients of your good deeds. The greatest gift is in giving freely without expecting anything in return. Even a small act of giving brings joy to another. Sometimes, our world needs a little inspiration to change people's lives and encourage them to do good to others. There are so many little ways to show you care. Reach out! It will warm your heart and the hearts of others. At the end of the day, you will realize how little you need, how much you have, and the value of the human connection. Pay it forward. You will not regret it.

A Kaleidoscope
Ways to Pay It Forward

Ponder this thought: "You may be only one person in this world, but to one person at one time, you are the world."

Anonymous

DATE _____

LET YOUR HEART SPEAK

JOURNALING . . .

KIND-HEARTEDNESS

BEING KIND-HEARTED IS A GRACIOUS WAY TO BRING JOY INTO OTHERS' LIVES AND ADD MEANING TO YOUR OWN. BEING KIND ALLOWS YOU TO COMMUNICATE BETTER. BE MORE COMPASSIONATE. AND BE A POSITIVE FORCE FOR GOOD. KINDNESS HAS ITS TRUSTWORTHY SOURCE DEEP WITHIN YOU. AND WHILE SOME PEOPLE ARE INNATELY KIND. KINDNESS IS SOMETHING EVERYONE CAN LEARN. THE DEFINITION OF KIND-HEARTED IS HAVING OR SHOWING A SYMPATHETIC OR EMPATHIC NATURE. KINDNESS BEGETS KINDNESS.

KINDNESS REFLECTS DEEP CARING FOR ALL BEINGS. PRACTICE

> " GOODNESS IS ABOUT CHARACTER. INTEGRITY. HONESTY. KINDNESS. GENEROSITY. MORAL COURAGE. AND THE LIKE. MORE THAN ANYTHING ELSE. IT IS ABOUT HOW WE TREAT OTHER PEOPLE.
>
> *Dennis Prager* "

KINDNESS AND GENEROSITY TOWARD OTHERS. GENUINE ACTS OF KINDNESS EXPECT NOTHING, COME WITH NO STRINGS ATTACHED, AND PLACE NO CONDITIONS ON ANYTHING DONE OR SAID. BEGIN BY BEING KIND TO YOURSELF. KINDNESS IS ABOUT LOANING SOMEONE YOUR STRENGTH INSTEAD OF REMINDING THEM OF THEIR WEAKNESS. CULTIVATE KINDNESS FOR THE GOOD OF YOUR HEALTH. KINDNESS PROMOTES A SENSE OF WELL-BEING THAT IMPROVES YOUR MENTAL STATE. BE KIND TO EVERYONE, NOT ONLY THOSE CLOSE TO YOU. BE A GOOD LISTENER. LISTEN WITH YOUR HEART. MAKE THE TIME TO PAY ATTENTION TO WHAT IS SHARED AND WHAT IS NOT SHARED. RESTING AT THE HEART OF KINDNESS ARE HAPPINESS, JOY, AND GRATITUDE. YOU WILL SEE THE GOOD IN OTHERS AND THE WORLD, RESTORING YOUR SENSE OF FAITH IN HUMANITY. BE FRIENDLY. GIVE COMPLIMENTS WHEN THEY ARE SINCERE. PRACTICE RANDOM ACTS OF KINDNESS.

WHEN YOU ARE KIND TO OTHERS, YOU ARE ALSO KIND TO YOURSELF. WILLIAM ARTHUR WARD REMINDS US. *A WARM SMILE IS THE UNIVERSAL LANGUAGE OF KINDNESS.* KINDNESS BEGINS WITH THE UNDERSTANDING THAT WE ALL STRUGGLE.

THERE ARE COUNTLESS WAYS OF SHOWING KINDNESS. THE ILLUSTRATION BELOW SUGGESTS RANDOM ACTS OF KINDNESS FOR YOU TO CONSIDER. WHEN YOU ACT WITH KIND-HEARTEDNESS, YOU RESPOND FROM THE GOODNESS OF YOUR HEART AND TOUCH THE HEART OF ANOTHER.

PONDER THIS THOUGHT: "EVERY WORD THAT CONVEYS ALTRUISM, AMIABILITY, CONSIDERATION, HELPFULNESS, CARE OR CONCERN HAS NO MEANING UNLESS IT IS FOLLOWED BY A GENUINE AND GRACEFUL ACTION DEVOID OF EXPECTING SOMETHING IN RETURN."

Freddy J. W. Park

LOVING KINDNESS IS A PROFOUND RECOGNITION
THAT OUR LIVES HAVE SOMETHING
TO DO WITH ONE ANOTHER.
THAT EVERYONE COUNTS.
EVERYONE MATTERS.

Sharon Salzberg

DATE _____

LET YOUR HEART SPEAK

JOURNALING . . .

LOVE TENDERLY

S T. JOHN OF THE CROSS REMINDS US, "*AT THE END OF LIFE, WE ARE GOING TO BE JUDGED BASED ON OUR LOVE FOR ONE ANOTHER.*" MOTHER TERESA LIVED THE WORDS OF ST. JOHN OF THE CROSS AND MADE IT HER MISSION TO EXTEND LOVING KINDNESS TO POOR, SICK, DYING, OR MARGINALIZED PEOPLE. TO LOVE AND BE LOVED IS WHAT LIFE IS ALL ABOUT. TO LOVE IS MUCH MORE THAN SHARING SPECIAL MOMENTS AND JOYFUL TIMES. IT IS ABOUT BEING A SUPPORTIVE PRESENCE IN GOOD AND CHALLENGING TIMES. WHEN YOU LOVE TENDERLY, YOU LOVE WITH GREAT SENSITIVITY TO THE NEEDS AND WANTS OF OTHERS. YOU DON'T COUNT THE COST. REACHING OUT IN LOVE IS AN EXPRESSION OF INTIMACY, A CONNECTION BUILT ON TRUST AND FRIENDSHIP.

IN 1965, "*WHAT THE WORLD NEEDS NOW IS LOVE,*" WITH LYRICS BY HAL DAVID AND MUSIC BY BURT BACHARACH, BECAME A POPULAR SONG. THE REFRAIN'S LAST LINE HAS A TIMELESS MESSAGE: "*LOVE IS NOT JUST FOR SOME, BUT FOR EVERYONE*" ECHOES OUR HEART'S DESIRE. WE CELEBRATE AND AFFIRM ALL

·WHAT THE WORLD NEEDS NOW
IS LOVE, SWEET LOVE
IT'S THE ONLY THING THAT THERE'S
JUST TOO LITTLE OF.
WHAT THE WORLD NEEDS NOW
IS LOVE SWEET LOVE
NO, NOT JUST FOR SOME
BUT FOR EVERYONE.

Fall in Love

WHAT YOU ARE IN LOVE WITH –

WHAT SEIZES YOUR IMAGINATION

WILL AFFECT EVERYTHING.

IT WILL DECIDE WHAT WILL GET YOU OUT OF BED

IN THE MORNING –

WHAT YOU DO WITH YOUR EVENINGS –

HOW YOU SPEND YOUR WEEKENDS –

WHAT YOU READ –

WHO YOU KNOW –

WHAT BREAKS YOUR HEART –

AND WHAT AMAZES YOU WITH JOY AND GRATITUDE.

FALL IN LOVE.

STAY IN LOVE.

AND IT WILL DECIDE EVERYTHING.

Attributed to Fr. Pedro Arrupe, SJ (1907-1991)

LIFE IS SHORT. NOW IS THE TIME TO GIVE YOURSELF PERMISSION TO LOVE AND BE LOVED AND FEEL THE INTIMACY OF THAT LIFE-SHARING, LIFE-SAVING CONNECTION.

PONDER THIS THOUGHT: "*BEING UNWANTED, UNLOVED, UNCARED FOR, FORGOTTEN BY EVERYBODY, I THINK IS A MUCH GREATER HUNGER, A MUCH GREATER POVERTY THAN THE PERSON WHO HAS NOTHING TO EAT.*"

St. Teresa of Calcutta

What the world needs now,

more than ever

is

LOVE sweet LOVE.

Date _____

LET YOUR HEART SPEAK

JOURNALING . . .

I

MISS

YOU

MISSING SOMEONE SPECIAL

D O YOU EVER JUST GET WAVES OF MISSING SOMEONE? DO YOU GO FOR A WHILE AND FEEL OKAY, AND THEN ALL OF A SUDDEN, YOUR HEART ACHES? MISSING SOMEONE IS YOUR HEART'S WAY OF REMINDING YOU THAT YOU LOVE SOMEONE SPECIAL. WHEN YOU LOSE SOMEONE YOU LOVE, IT TAKES TIME TO SHIFT FROM LIVING WITHOUT THEM TO LIVING WITH THE LOVE THEY LEFT BEHIND.

MY DEAR SISTER, ANN, DIED AFTER A LONG BATTLE WITH CANCER. HER DIAGNOSIS DEVASTATED ME. I HAD LOST OTHER LOVED ONES, BUT THE THOUGHT OF LOSING ANN SEEMED UNBEARABLE. SHE WAS MORE THAN A SISTER TO ME. ANN WAS MY BEST FRIEND, MY CONFIDANT, MY CHEERLEADER, AND MY ROLE MODEL. ANN AND I SHARED A SPECIAL BOND THAT UNITED US IN A RELATIONSHIP OF MUTUAL LOVE. ANN WAS AFFECTIONATELY CALLED *"LADYBUGS."* TINY LADYBUGS APPEAR ON SOME OF THE PAGES AS A WAY OF HONORING MEMORIES OF A VERY SPECIAL, GENTLE PERSON, MY SISTER, ANN. WHEN I SEE A TINY LADYBUG, MY THOUGHTS GO IMMEDIATELY TO ANN, AND I SMILE, SOMETIMES THROUGH TEARS.

I KEEP HAVING LONGING THOUGHTS OF ANN. THERE ARE MANY REMINDERS OF HER ALL AROUND ME. FOR MONTHS AFTER ANN'S DEATH, I UNCONSCIOUSLY CRAVED HER FAVORITE FOODS, WORE THE CLOTHES SHE LIKED, AND TRIED TO ADOPT HER MUSIC AND CRAFTS STYLE. I WANTED TO HAVE VIVID DREAMS OF HER, FEARING I WOULD FORGET HER UNIQUE QUALITIES. REMEMBERING ANN OFTEN BRINGS TEARS TO MY EYES, TEARS OF LOVE AND GRATITUDE FOR THE BLESSING OF HAVING A WONDERFUL SISTER IN MY LIFE. HER SPIRIT IS VERY MUCH ALIVE IN MY HEART, BUT THERE IS STILL A HOLE IN MY HEART., A LACK OF JOY. LIVING WITHOUT ANN IS DIFFICULT AND SOMETIMES SEEMS TO LACK DIRECTION. SURVIVING AND TRYING TO MAKE SENSE OF REALITY ADDS A DIMENSION OF NUMBNESS TO MY EXISTENCE. TIME SEEMS TO MOVE AT A DIFFERENT PACE. I FEEL AN ALONENESS AND EMPTINESS THAT MAKES ME FEEL ABANDONED. THE

PASSAGE OF TIME HELPS ME LIVE WITH THE REALITY THAT MY SISTER IS NOW WITH GOD. I PRAY FOR ANN AND TO ANN. MY PEACE COMES IN BELIEVING I WILL ONE DAY BE UNITED WITH HER. UNTIL THEN...ANN'S GOODNESS MOTIVATES ME TO LIVE MY BEST *QUALITY OF LIFE*, AND CELEBRATE THE SPECIAL MEMORIES OF OUR SHARED TIME TOGETHER. THERE IS LITTLE SOLACE ON THE PATH OF GRIEF. EVEN THOUGH GRIEVING IS NECESSARY FOR HEALING, IT IS NOT EASY. TAKE GENTLE CARE OF YOURSELF AS YOU TAKE THE TIME TO GRIEVE.

"THOSE WE LOVE AND LOSE ARE ALWAYS CONNECTED BY HEARTSTRINGS INTO INFINITY.
Terri Goodlette"

DEATH IS SO FINAL. WHY DOES THE SEPARATION HURT SO MUCH? WE TEND TO DO EVERYTHING TO HOLD ON TO MEMORIES. YET, SAD FEELINGS LINGER IN OUR GRIEF. FOR MONTHS AFTER A DEATH, IT IS NORMAL TO QUESTION "*WHY.*" IN TIME, OUR PRAYER BECOMES ONE OF GRATITUDE FOR THE GIFT OF LOVING SOMEONE VERY SPECIAL. THE CONVERSION FROM RAW GRIEF TO ACCEPTANCE HAPPENS WHEN WE CAN SMILE AS MEMORIES OF OUR LOVED ONES FLOOD OUR THOUGHTS. AS WE CONTINUE TO HEAL, THE HEARTACHE LESSENS, AND WE BEGIN TO REFOCUS ON CHERISHING THE PRECIOUS MEMORIES.

YOUR LIFE IS FOREVER CHANGED WHEN SOMEONE YOU LOVE DIES. THOSE THAT GO BEFORE YOU WILL NEVER AGAIN BE PART OF YOUR EARTHLY JOURNEY. WHEN YOU

PROCESS YOUR PAIN AND GRIEF, YOU CAN HOLD ON TO THE MEMORIES THAT YOU HOLD DEAR. IT IS HARD TO LIVE WITHOUT SOMEONE WHO GAVE YOU SO MUCH TO REMEMBER. YET, THERE IS A SPECIAL STRENGTH REVEALED IN GROWING THROUGH WHAT YOU GO THROUGH. AS DIFFICULT AS IT IS, IT HELPS YOU BE COMPASSIONATE TO ANOTHER'S GRIEVING HEART.

THE LOSS OF A LOVED ONE WALKS BESIDE YOU EVERY DAY. THE INITIAL DAYS OF FEELING THE LOSS ARE LIKE WALKING IN A VALLEY OF TEARS. HEARTACHE CAN BE WORSE THAN ANY PHYSICAL PAIN. THE ACHE TOUCHES YOUR SOUL, AND CRIES IN INCONSOLABLE GRIEF. IT IS UNLIKE ANY OTHER FEELING. YET, THIS HALLOWED PLACE IS THE FIRST AND MOST DIFFICULT JUNCTION ON THE ROAD TO FINDING LIGHT, PEACE, AND ACCEPTANCE. GRIEVING OFFERS NO DETOUR.

IF YOU MISS SOMEONE SPECIAL TODAY, TAKE A BREAK AND PAUSE TO REMEMBER THE QUALITIES YOU ADMIRED AND LOVED ABOUT THAT PERSON. THEN, SMILE AS YOU CARRY THEIR CHERISHED MEMORIES IN THE FULLNESS OF YOUR HEART.

PONDER THIS THOUGHT: "DEATH LEAVES A HEARTACHE NO ONE CAN HEAL; LOVE LEAVES A MEMORY NO ONE CAN STEAL."

Mary Robinson

Absence

Sometimes I know the way
You walk. up over the bay:
It is a wind from that far sea
That blows the fragrance of your hair to me.

Or in this garden when the breeze
Touches my trees
To stir their dreaming shadows on the grass
I see you pass.

In sheltered beds. the heart of every rose
Serenely sleeps to-night. As shut as those
Your guarded heart: as safe as they fomr the beat.
Beat
Of hooves that tread dropped roses in the street.

Turn never again
On these eyes blind with a wild rain
Your eyes: they were stars to me.—
There are things stars may not see.

But call. call. and though Christ stands
Still with scarred hands
Over my mouth. I must answer. So
I will come—He shall let me go!

Charlotte Mew
1869-1928

Date _____

LET YOUR HEART SPEAK

JOURNALING . . .

No Regrets?

A S A HOSPICE CHAPLAIN, I LEARNED MUCH ABOUT REGRET. I WAS SURPRISED AT HOW MANY OF MY PATIENTS GOT TO THE END OF THEIR LIVES, REGRETTING THE CHOICES THEY MADE. THEY WERE REMORSEFUL ABOUT THEIR BROKEN RELATIONSHIPS AND UNFULFILLED DREAMS. SOME HAD FEELINGS OF GUILT AND RESENTMENT THAT THEY NEVER RESOLVED. MANY FOUND THE COURAGE IN THEIR LAST DAYS TO ASK FOR AND OFFER FORGIVENESS. MY MOST PROFOUND MOMENTS WERE WITNESSING THE PEACE AND JOY OF LOVE RESTORED THROUGH ACTS OF FORGIVENESS. THEIR GREATEST REGRET WAS WAITING SO LONG TO SEEK FORGIVENESS AND MEND BROKEN RELATIONSHIPS. IT WAS BEAUTIFUL TO OBSERVE HEALED RELATIONSHIPS. SEEING THE JOY OF LOVED ONES RECONNECTED AFTER A LONG AND PAINFUL HIATUS WAS HEART-WARMING.

> " NOBODY GETS TO LIVE LIFE BACKWARD. LOOK AHEAD. THAT IS WHERE YOUR FUTURE LIES. "
>
> *Ann Landers*

More than likely, everyone will experience feelings of regret at least once in their lifetime. You can do several things to accept and overcome your guilt and shame, so they do not restrict your *QUALITY OF LIFE*. It is a blessing when remorse becomes a lesson learned. Do I have regrets? I do. Some were because of my poor choices; some were because of circumstances that negatively impacted my life, inflicting emotional suffering. I sought therapy to process my pain. My resolve has been to live a peaceful and happy life. We don't know how much time we have on this earth. Each day is a blessing filled with hope and promise. Forgiveness of self and others is a powerful healing agent. Shannon L. Alder imparts: *"One of the greatest regrets in life is being what others would want you to be, rather than being yourself."* Not wanting to hurt or disappoint others can keep us from sharing who we are and the desires of our hearts.

When I think about seeking peace, the Serenity Prayer, written by American theologian Reinhold Niebuhr, offers comfort and hope:

Learn from your mistakes and believe you deserve a good life. Your past is history and does not have to enslave you with guilt for the rest of your life. Greet each new day with a positive attitude. Tread gently and seek a grateful heart. Let go of resentments and grudges. Forgive yourself and others. Be yourself. Your authentic self is your best self.

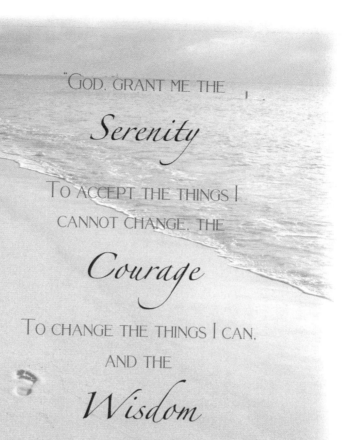

"GOD, GRANT ME THE

Serenity

TO ACCEPT THE THINGS I
CANNOT CHANGE, THE

Courage

TO CHANGE THE THINGS I CAN,
AND THE

Wisdom

TO KNOW THE DIFFERENCE."

Ponder this thought: "There is a strange comfort in knowing that no matter what happens today, the sun will rise again tomorrow."

Aaron Lauritsen

"THE SOUL WOULD HAVE
NO RAINBOW
IF THE EYES
HAD NO TEARS."

Native American proverb

DATE

LET YOUR HEART SPEAK

JOURNALING . . .

Be Hopeful

Optimism:
Finding Hope
During Difficult Times

Having a hopeful attitude during a difficult time usually predicts a better outcome. Being optimistic helps you cope with the challenges that come your way. It enables you to imagine affirmative results. A bright outlook gives you the energy to focus on the positive instead of dwelling on the harsh negatives. Optimism is an inclination to put a favorable outlook on actions and events, expecting a possible resolution. You can aspire to imagine positive results and set aside the pessimistic predictions by being optimistic. A growing number of scientific studies suggest optimistic people tend to live longer and have better physical and mental health than those with a negative outlook.

All of my adult life, I have enjoyed the reputation of being positive. It is a gift that allows me to be optimistic and look to the brighter side.

EVEN IN THE DARKEST TIMES. THE WORD *HOPE* HAS BEEN MY MANTRA MOST OF MY LIFE. FRIENDS OFTEN TEASE ME BECAUSE MY BLOOD TYPE IS B POSITIVE (B+). A GOOD MATCH FOR MY POSITIVE ATTITUDE. I ALWAYS BELIEVE THERE IS A WAY THINGS WILL WORK OUT. IT MAY NOT BE EASY. BUT ALL WILL BE WELL WITH CREATIVITY. INGENUITY. AND TRUST IN GOD.

ZACH CUTLER. AN ENTREPRENEUR. SUGGESTS THE FOLLOWING FIVE BENEFITS TO BEING OPTIMISTIC:

1. *SEE FAILURE AS A NEW START.* FAILURE IS NOT THE END. INSTEAD. IT IS OFTEN THE BEGINNING OF SOMETHING GREAT. WHEN THINGS ARE GOOD. YOU COAST ALONG. WHEN THINGS GO BAD. YOUR WORLD GETS SHAKEN UP. REQUIRING YOU TO GROW. SEE NEW WAYS. AND START AFRESH.

2. *BE EXPANSIVE.* PESSIMISM MAKES YOU SHY AWAY FROM NEW AND ADVENTUROUS THINGS. OPTIMISM OPENS YOU TO NEW IDEAS. FREEING YOU TO CONSIDER NEW OPTIONS. POSITIVELY CHANGING YOUR LIFE.

3. *GET HEALTHY.* OPTIMISTS ARE GENERALLY HAPPIER AND LESS STRESSED. AND HAVE HEALTHIER HEARTS. FOCUSING ON THE POSITIVE IMPROVES YOUR WELL-BEING. IT MOTIVATES YOU TO TAKE CARE OF YOUR HEALTH.

4. *SPREAD POSITIVE VIBES.* OPTIMISM IS CONTAGIOUS. HAVING AN UPBEAT ATTITUDE CAN INSPIRE OTHERS. ATTITUDE IS EVERYTHING.

5. *IT IS THE BEST CHOICE.* THERE IS NO BETTER ALTERNATIVE TO OPTIMISM. PESSIMISM DOESN'T ACHIEVE MUCH. EVERYTHING WON'T ALWAYS BE GREAT. BUT OPTIMISM HELPS YOU SEE NEW OPPORTUNITIES AND LEARN FROM DIFFERENT SITUATIONS. SO IT PAYS TO BE OPTIMISTIC.

HOPE PLAYS A HUGE ROLE IN HAVING A POSITIVE OUTLOOK ON LIFE. IT GIVES YOU THE MOTIVATION TO CHANGE AND LIVE LIFE FULLY. WITH HOPE IN YOUR HEART. YOU CAN DREAM AND BELIEVE IN A BETTER FUTURE. YOU CAN DRAW ON YOUR INNER RESILIENCE AND YOUR CONVICTION THAT YOUR SPIRIT OF HOPEFULNESS WILL CARRY YOU FORWARD. FINDING HOPE HELPS YOU DRAW ON THE POSITIVITY OF AFFIRMING PEOPLE. PLACES. AND THINGS. LIFE DOES NOT HAVE TO BE PERFECT TO BE BEAUTIFUL. STRIVE FOR A PEACEFUL SPIRIT. APPRECIATE THE SMALL MOMENTS OF HAPPINESS THAT TAKE YOU BY SURPRISE. EMILY DICKINSON'S POEM GIVES AN IMAGE TO HOPE. A WORD DEEPLY FELT BUT HARD TO DESCRIBE:

Hope Is The Thing With Feathers

"Hope" is the thing with feathers –
That perches in the soul –
And sings the tune without the words –
And never stops at all –

The sweetest – in the Gale – is heard –
And sore must be the storm –
That could abash the little Bird
That kept so many warm –

I've heard it in the chilliest land –
And on the Strangest Sea –
Yet – never – in Extremity.
It asked a crumb – of me

As you walk through your day and go about your daily activities. Be optimistic and remember to:

Have

Only

Positive

Expectations.

Ponder this thought: "Now I know in part; then I shall know fully, even as I am fully known. And now these three remain: faith, hope, and love; and the greatest of these is love."

1 Corinthians 13:1

Date _____

LET YOUR HEART SPEAK

Journaling . . .

PERSISTENCE:
DON'T GIVE UP

D O YOU EVER FEEL YOU ARE AT A CROSSROADS IN YOUR LIFE WHERE YOU ARE COASTING AND LIVING WITH UNPLEASANT REALITIES BECAUSE YOU DON'T HAVE THE ENERGY OR WHEREWITHAL TO DO SOMETHING ABOUT IT? SOMETIMES IT IS MUCH EASIER TO ACCEPT THE INEVITABLE RATHER THAN TACKLE THE HURDLES OF JOURNEYING ON A PATH TO A MORE MEANINGFUL, PEACEFUL LIFE. INITIATING A CHANGE IN YOUR OUTLOOK, ATTITUDE, AND BEHAVIOR CAN BE DAUNTING, BUT THE REWARD IS PRICELESS: YOUR HAPPINESS.

IF YOU COULD REWRITE YOUR LIFE SCRIPT, WHAT WOULD IT REFLECT? DO NOT LET COMPLACENCY, FEAR, AND UNCERTAINTY CRIPPLE YOU FROM CARING ENOUGH ABOUT YOUR HAPPINESS TO TAKE THE NEXT STEP AND BEGIN THE JOURNEY TO INITIATE POSITIVE CHANGE IN YOUR LIFE.

THE TIME TO ACT IS NOW! CONSIDER TAKING STEPS TO MAKE CHANGE HAPPEN INSTEAD OF JUST WISHING FOR IT. TAKE THE TIME TO ASSESS YOUR SITUATION AND TAKE RESPONSIBILITY FOR CREATING THE DESIRED CHANGE. SOMETIMES THE CHANGE

IS MORE ABOUT YOUR MENTAL ATTITUDE THAN A DRASTIC LIFESTYLE CHANGE. PRAY FOR THE WISDOM TO CLEARLY SEE WHAT MODIFICATIONS IN YOUR LIFE WILL GENERATE PEACE AND HAPPINESS. IF NECESSARY, SEEK PROFESSIONAL AND SPIRITUAL GUIDANCE TO VALIDATE YOUR GOALS AND THEN WORK ON A REALISTIC PLAN TO ACCOMPLISH YOUR LIFE-ALTERING DREAM. WALK WITH PATIENCE AND CONFIDENCE TOWARD YOUR GOAL. NO ONE ELSE CAN MAKE CHOICES FOR YOU, AND NO ONE SHOULD. IT TAKES COURAGE, PATIENCE, AND PERSEVERANCE TO SEEK PEACE AND CONTENTMENT. BE PERSISTENT, INVESTING THE NECESSARY TIME TO ESTABLISH YOUR NEW REALITY. FOR EXAMPLE, YOUR PLAN MAY BE AS SIMPLE AS COMMITTING TO MEDITATION EACH DAY FOR TEN MINUTES, DECIDING TO LEAVE A TOXIC OR ABUSIVE RELATIONSHIP, OR LEAVING A JOB THAT DRAINS YOU OF YOUR DIGNITY AND SELF-WORTH.

PARTICIPATE IN THE PROCESS OF ACHIEVING YOUR GOAL. THE PROCESS DOESN'T HAPPEN AUTOMATICALLY. BUT, THE LONGER YOU PERSIST, THE MORE LIKELY YOU WILL CREATE THE LIFE YOU DESERVE. AND, YES, YOU DO DESERVE A WONDERFUL LIFE FILLED WITH HAPPINESS, JOY, AND PEACE.

CHALLENGING TIMES ARE PART OF THE UNFOLDING MYSTERY OF LIFE. DISAPPOINTMENTS AND TRAGIC NEWS MIGHT INTERRUPT THE NORMAL RHYTHM OF YOUR LIFE. YET, EVEN THOUGH THE DIFFICULT TIMES FEEL LIKE THEY WILL BREAK YOU, KNOW YOU POSSESS AN INCREDIBLE INNER STRENGTH THAT CAN PUSH YOU FORWARD. HAVING THE MINDSET TO PERSIST HELPS YOU TO OVERCOME YOUR FEARS AND DOUBTS. WHILE INTENTIONALLY WORKING TOWARD A SIGNIFICANT CHANGE, TAKE GENTLE CARE OF YOURSELF. TAKE THE TIME TO QUIET YOURSELF. JACK KORNFIELD SHARES, *PART OF THE ART OF QUIETING YOURSELF IS ALSO TO HONOR THE TEARS THAT YOU CARRY.* BE PERSISTENT IN FINDING GRATITUDE FOR THE BLESSINGS IN YOUR LIFE. EVERY NEW DAY IS A NEW BEGINNING. HONOR THE TEARS OF YESTERDAY AND LOOK TO THIS NEW DAY WITH A GRATEFUL HEART. IN THE QUIET OF YOUR BEING, DECIDE WHAT YOU CAN DO TODAY TO IMPROVE

> " THE ONE WHO FALLS AND GETS UP IS STRONGER THAN THE ONE WHO NEVER TRIED. DO NOT FEAR FAILURE BUT RATHER FEAR NOT TRYING.
>
> *Roy T Bennett* "

YOUR *QUALITY OF LIFE*. LIVE TODAY KNOWING GOD'S GRACE ACCOMPANIES YOU. REMEMBER, YOU ARE STRONGER THAN YOU THINK, WISER THAN YOU BELIEVE, AND MORE RESILIENT THAN YOU EVER IMAGINED. DON'T GIVE UP ON YOUR QUEST TO SEEK A PEACEFUL LIFE.

WHAT CHANGES DO YOU WISH TO MAKE IN YOUR LIFE TO EXPERIENCE GREATER PEACE AND HAPPINESS?

PONDER THIS THOUGHT: "YOU DESERVE A LOVE THAT CAN CONQUER ALL, EVEN THE HARDEST TEMPTATIONS AND THE MOST UNBEARABLE DISCOURAGEMENT. A LOVE THAT WILL KEEP YOU SAFE."

Raquel's Manuel

DON'T GIVE UP

"BELIEVE YOU CAN AND YOU ARE HALFWAY THERE"

Theodore Roosevelt

DATE _____

LET YOUR HEART SPEAK

JOURNALING . . .

QUALITY OF LIFE

Q UALITY OF LIFE IS ABOUT HAVING SATISFACTION AND LIVING LIFE TO THE FULLEST. IT HAS TO DO WITH MANAGING YOUR HEALTH, WELL-BEING, AND HAPPINESS AND HOW THESE QUALITIES BECOME INTEGRATED WITH YOUR SPIRITUAL AND PHILOSOPHICAL VALUES. *QUALITY OF LIFE* IS NOT JUST ABOUT THE ABSENCE OF DISEASE BUT THE INTENTIONALITY OF MAKING EVERY EFFORT TO LIVE A GOOD LIFE EVERY DAY.

IF LIFE WERE TO CHANGE DRASTICALLY FOR YOU TODAY, WHAT WOULD YOU HOLD MOST DEAR? WHAT WOULD BE MOST IMPORTANT TO YOU?

YOUR LIFE BECOMES RICHER WHEN YOU CHALLENGE YOURSELF TO REFLECT ON THE CHOICES YOU MAKE, THOUGHTS YOU THINK, AND WORDS YOU SAY. SOMETIMES YOU MAY FORGET YOU HAVE SOMETHING TO OFFER OTHERS THAT ONLY YOU CAN GIVE. THE MORE YOU CAN CONNECT WITH OUR GIFTS, TALENTS, AND QUALITIES AND LET THEM SHINE, THE BETTER YOUR LIFE BECOMES. YOUR *QUALITY OF LIFE* IS ABOUT SPREADING YOUR UNIQUE MESSAGE, WISDOM, AND ENCOURAGEMENT. IN THESE WAYS, YOU NURTURE

AND CULTIVATE YOUR RELATIONSHIPS THROUGH YOUR ACTIONS AND WORDS. YOU MAKE INVESTMENTS
IN YOUR RELATIONSHIPS BY LISTENING, REACHING OUT, AND TELLING OTHERS YOU CARE. CULTIVATING DEPTH IN YOUR RELATIONSHIPS COMES FROM BEING WILLING TO LEARN FROM OTHERS, NOTING THE UNIQUE VALUE THEY OFFER, AND EXPRESSING YOUR GRATITUDE.

LIVING YOUR BEST *QUALITY OF LIFE* MEANS LETTING GO OF THE SMALL STUFF, SETTING LOVING BOUNDARIES, SHOWING EMPATHY AND UNDERSTANDING, GIVING SELFLESSLY TO OTHERS, AND REMINDING YOUR FAMILY AND FRIENDS HOW MUCH YOU LOVE AND APPRECIATE THEM.

ASK YOURSELF, WHAT BRINGS ME JOY? AM I LIVING MY LIFE TO THE FULLEST? WHAT MAKES ME LAUGH? HUMILITY IS ACCEPTING WHO YOU ARE WITH YOUR GOD-GIVEN TALENTS AND A REALISTIC AWARENESS OF YOUR ABILITIES. THE CHOICES YOU MAKE DETERMINE YOUR *QUALITY OF LIFE.* YOU CAN CHOOSE TO CELEBRATE AND LIVE A LIFE FILLED WITH MEANING BY MAKING CHOICES THAT ECHO HARMONY AND BALANCE. TO DO SO, YOU NEED TO EMBRACE ALL THAT YOU ARE AND HAVE A SENSE OF PURPOSE TO LIVE EACH DAY WITH A PEACEFUL CALMNESS.

> 66
> THE REAL THINGS HAVEN'T CHANGED.
> IT IS STILL BEST TO BE HONEST AND TRUTHFUL:
> TO MAKE THE MOST OF WHAT WE HAVE.
> TO BE HAPPY WITH THE SIMPLE PLEASURES AND HAVE COURAGE WHEN THINGS GO WRONG.
> *Laura Ingalls Wilder*
> 99

CHOOSING TO BE HEALTHY MEANS FOLLOWING A PROTOCOL THAT IMPROVES YOUR HEALTH. WHAT YOU EAT, WHEN YOU SLEEP, WHEN YOU EXERCISE, WHEN YOU PAUSE TO SLOW DOWN AND MEDITATE, HOW YOU SPEND YOUR FREE TIME – ALL OF THESE ARE CHOICES THAT AFFECT YOUR OVERALL HEALTH AND WELL-BEING. MODERATION AND BALANCE HELP YOU AVOID EXTREMES. TAKING TIME FOR YOURSELF IS NOT BEING SELFISH. IT IS GIVING YOU TIME TO REJUVENATE AND REPLENISH YOUR ENERGY RESERVOIR.

YOUR BEST *QUALITY OF LIFE* EXPERIENCE IS YOUR ABILITY TO LOOK DEEP INSIDE YOURSELF AND FIND THE QUALITIES NEEDED TO LIVE YOUR BOLDEST DREAMS. *QUALITY OF LIFE* IS ABOUT FINDING A HAPPY BALANCE. WILL YOU CHOOSE TO MAKE THE REST OF YOUR LIFE THE BEST OF YOUR LIFE. SHARING WARMTH. KINDNESS. AND COMPASSION. A LIFE THAT IS MEANINGFUL AND MORE PEACEFUL – HAPPIER? PAUSE! ENJOY LIFE'S SIMPLE PLEASURES.

PONDER THIS THOUGHT: "IN THE END. IT'S NOT THE YEARS IN YOUR LIFE THAT COUNT. IT'S THE LIFE IN YOUR YEARS."

Abraham Lincoln

Your Quality of Life is enriched when:

You Love
You Believe
You Are You
You can forgive
You say "I love you."
You put others first
You exercise to stay fit
You are kind to yourself
You can let go of past hurts
You take "Me" time to recharge
You celebrate another's success
You spend quality time with friends
You enjoy the gift of time to slow down
You see God in rising and setting of the sun
You can trust in God enough to stop worrying
You keep trying to balance back after a setback
You reach out in loving-kindness to those struggling
You are grateful to those who have reached out to you
You choose to risk and stretch your limits to enjoy adventure
You live daily with a grateful heart and see the good in others.

Marguerite P. Gilner

Date _____

Let your heart speak

Journaling . . .

"BE STILL . . .
AND
KNOW
I AM GOD."

Psalm 46:10

DATE _____

LET YOUR HEART SPEAK

SEARCH THE HORIZON

AT CERTAIN TIMES IN OUR LIVES, WE COME TO A PIVOTAL POINT WHEN WE RECOGNIZE THE NEED TO SLOW DOWN AND TAKE THE SPACE TO SEEK A MORE PURPOSEFUL LIFE. WE ARE RESPONDING TO A CALL FOR A QUEST FOR DEEPER MEANING. WHEN THAT TIME COMES, WE TRANSCEND WHAT WE KNOW AND EMBARK ON AN ADVENTURE TO EXPLORE THE VAST POSSIBILITIES BEYOND OUR HORIZON.

FOCUSING ON YOUR QUEST, YOU BECOME HUMBLER AND WISER. TAKING THE TIME TO SEARCH MAKES YOU MORE CONSCIOUS OF THE CRUCIAL PLACE OF GENEROSITY AND KINDNESS IN YOUR EVERYDAY LIFE. SEARCHING OFTEN BEGINS WITH THAT VOICE INSIDE YOU THAT SAYS YOU CAN BE WHAT YOU IMAGINE. BUT, YOU HAVE TO WORK, SACRIFICE, PLAN, AND BE PATIENT AS YOU SEEK A MORE GENUINE SENSE OF SELF.

AS YOU PRAYERFULLY ENGAGE IN YOUR PURSUIT OF HAPPINESS, WHICH INCLUDES NOT ONLY SATISFYING YOUR OWN NEEDS BUT BEING AWARE OF THE NEEDS OF OTHERS, FINDING FULFILLMENT IN REACHING OUT TO THE COMMUNITY AND THE

WORLD. IT WOULD BE BEST IF YOU BECAME MORE OUTWARD-FOCUSED TO FIND PEACE WITHIN. IN GIVING, YOU WILL FIND FULFILLMENT AND SATISFACTION. AS ST. FRANCIS TELLS US, *"IT IS IN GIVING THAT WE RECEIVE."*

WHILE REACHING OUT TO OTHERS, BE CAREFUL ABOUT BEING EMOTIONALLY DRAINED YOURSELF, LEAVING YOU INCAPABLE OF RESPONDING TO ANOTHER'S NEEDS. TAKE THE TIME TO REFUEL, REST AND PRAYERFULLY DISCERN WAYS TO USE YOUR GIFTS AND TALENTS TO HELP OTHERS. WHEN YOU ARE READY TO OFFER A HELPING HAND, BE CAUTIOUS NOT TO CRITICIZE, JUDGE, OR EVEN ATTEMPT TO WONDER HOW THOSE IN NEED GET INTO SUCH A STATE OF AFFAIRS. LET *"THERE BUT FOR THE GRACE OF GOD, GO I"* RING LOUD AND CLEAR. THIS AGE-OLD PROVERBIAL PHRASE REMINDS YOU THAT YOUR SITUATION COULD QUICKLY CHANGE FROM GOOD FORTUNE TO A HARDSHIP, PUTTING YOURSELF IN THEIR SITUATION. STRIVE TO BE EMPATHIC AND RESPECT THE LESS FORTUNATE WITH KIND AND GENTLE COMPASSION.

> 66
> THE MEANING OF LIFE IS TO FIND YOUR GIFT.
> THE PURPOSE OF LIFE IS TO GIVE IT AWAY.
> *Pablo Picasso*
> 99

LOOKING BACK OVER YOUR LIFE HELPS YOU APPRECIATE WHY YOU MADE YOUR CHOICES, AND IT ALLOWS YOU TO EVALUATE THE PRICE YOU PAID FOR THOSE CHOICES. IT IS A HUMBLING TASK, BUT IT PROVIDES INSIGHT INTO HOW YOU DEAL WITH CIRCUMSTANCES, STRESSORS, AND TENSIONS IN YOUR LIFE. IN ADDITION, BEING ABLE TO FORGIVE YOURSELF FOR YOUR UNHEALTHY CHOICES HELPS YOU LOVE AND FORGIVE OTHERS.

YOUR SEARCH IS NEVER OVER; YOUR QUEST CONTINUES. KEEP ASKING YOURSELF THE QUESTION: *"WHAT DO I VALUE IN LIFE?"* AS YOU BECOME MORE INSIGHTFUL, YOU WILL STRIVE FOR A GREATER SENSE OF GOODNESS, TRUTH, LOVE, AND HAPPINESS. YOU MAY STUMBLE AND SOMETIMES FALL SHORT OF YOUR ASPIRATIONS IN YOUR QUEST. WHEN YOU STUMBLE, YOU NEED TO MAKE THAT A PART OF YOUR DANCE. IT TAKES A LONG TIME TO LEARN TO WALTZ THROUGH LIFE'S CHALLENGES AND STILL DANCE TO THE BEAT OF A GRATEFUL HEART. TOMORROW IS ANOTHER DAY TO BEGIN ANEW WITH ENERGY AND VITALITY TO SEARCH YOUR HORIZON. SOMETIMES YOUR SEARCH GUIDES YOU TO THE UNCHARTED DREAMS THAT COME TRUE. IT MAKES YOUR SEARCH

REWARDING AND WORTH THE EFFORT. EVERY DAY YOU MAKE CHOICES THAT IMPACT HOW YOU LIVE AND INTERACT WITH OTHERS. TAKE ADVANTAGE OF ALL THAT LIES ON THE HORIZON FOR YOU. YOU HAVE OPTIONS, AND IT IS NEVER TOO LATE TO EXPLORE THEM. YOU DESERVE A BALANCED, HAPPY LIFE.

CONTINUE TO BE OPEN-MINDED AND FLEXIBLE. YOUR PRIORITIES WILL SHIFT OVER TIME. WHAT WAS IMPORTANT A FEW YEARS AGO MAY NO LONGER BE RELEVANT. AS YOU SEARCH YOUR HORIZON, YOU WILL DISCOVER NEW DIMENSIONS TO YOUR QUEST FOR MEANING AND PURPOSE. AS YOU TAKE THE TIME TO UNDERSTAND YOUR PAST AND INTENTIONALLY DECIDE ON THE DIRECTION OF YOUR FUTURE, CONTINUE TO REACH OUT TO BE A BLESSING TO OTHERS.

PONDER THIS THOUGHT: "JUST BEYOND THE HORIZON OF THE SO-CALLED IMPOSSIBLE IS INFINITE POSSIBILITY."

Bryant McGill

- 119 -

SEARCH

Search your heart

Search your mind

Search you dreams

Search your thoughts

Search your soul

Keep searching

Until you find love

Keep Loving

Until you find yourself

Keep yourself submerged in LOVE

Kenneth Maswabi

DATE _____

LET YOUR HEART SPEAK

Those who trust in God
will find new strength.
They will soar
high on wings
like eagles.

Isaiah 40:31

TAKE GENTLE CARE

TAKE GENTLE CARE AS YOU PLACE YOUR HAND OVER YOUR HEART AND RECALL WHAT IS IMPORTANT FOR YOU. PRAY WITH GRATITUDE FOR YOUR MANY BLESSINGS. SET REALISTIC BOUNDARIES. YOU ARE IN CHARGE. AND YOU GET TO DECIDE HOW YOU LIVE TODAY. AND TOMORROW. WHEN THINGS ARE DIFFERENT. YOU CAN CHOOSE AGAIN. BEAUTIFUL THINGS HAPPEN EVEN AMID TRAGEDY AND CHAOS. SOMETIMES YOUR CONSCIENCE IS DEAFENING WITH GOOD ADVICE. YOU HAVE A CHOICE TO EITHER LISTEN OR IGNORE YOUR INNER VOICE. LISTENING AND RESPONDING BRING INNER PEACE. STAY THE COURSE. STAY STRONG.

A SIMPLE AND UNCLUTTERED LIFESTYLE IS THE WAY BACK TO LOVE. THE WAY BACK TO HEALTH. AND THE WAY BACK TO YOU. REMEMBER. YOU ARE SPECIAL! IF YOU WANT TO FEEL HEALTHIER. COME BACK TO HEALTHY HABITS WITHOUT GUILT FOR LETTING THEM GO. COMING BACK IS YOUR CONNECTION TO HOPE. THERE IS HEALING IN HOPE.

When I was a graduate student at George Washington University, I had a professor who stayed in touch with his students by frequent emails. Paul Francis Tschudi was on GWU's faculty in the Master of Health Science and End of Life Care program. He was the faculty's connection, always available to his students. Paul ended his emails with the complimentary closing *"TAKE GENTLE CARE."* It meant much more to me than the typical TAKE CARE closing. I have adopted his coined phrase because of its caring implications.

Not surprisingly, Paul Tschudi was a dedicated professor who had a passion for alleviating humankind's suffering. Tragically, Paul died in a house fire a year. His final Facebook posting sums up this book's purpose and is a testimony to Paul's life mission.

Paul, thank you for making a difference in my life and the lives of many. You were an enlightened soul, a humble person, a mentor, a professor, and a treasured friend. You made the world a better place. May you soar high on eagle's wings!

Ponder this thought: "Be healing with your words, be tender with your words, be gentle with your words and watch your words bring gentle, tender healing in the hearts of others."

Heather Wolf

Paul Tschudi's Last Facebook Post

Note to Self

"What is my purpose in life?" I asked the void.
"What if I told you that you fulfilled it when
you took an extra hour to talk to a kid about his life?"
said the voice.
"Or when you paid for that young couple
in the restaurant?
Or when you saved that dog in traffic?
Or when you tied your father's shoes for him?"
"Your problem is that you equate your purpose
with goal-based achievement.
The Universe isn't interested in your achievements...
just your heart.
When you choose to act out of kindness,
compassion and love,
you are already aligned with your true purpose."
"No Need To Look Any Further."

Anonymous

YOU ARE STRONG, YET FRAGILE. YOU ARE ALSO VERY HUMAN.

TAKE CARE OF YOURSELF TO CELEBRATE AND ENJOY LIFE.

IN OUR HECTIC WORLD,

LISTEN TO HEAR THE SOUND OF YOUR HEART.

LET YOUR HEART SPEAK

OF WHAT IS IMPORTANT TO YOU.

JUST LIKE A DELICATE ROSE, FRAGRANT, AND SO BEAUTIFUL,

SO ARE YOU.

LET YOUR BEAUTY SHINE.

DATE _____

LET YOUR HEART SPEAK

JOURNALING . . .

Understanding
"I Am Sorry"

Saying *I Am Sorry* is an expression of remorse and an outreach for healing. Even before the uttering of the words, soul-searching begins. Processing your feelings and emotions is vital to sort out the circumstances that led to the hurt. You need to struggle with your rationalizations, excuses, justifications to get down to an honest appraisal. Yet, there comes a time when you have to admit that you were wrong, and it was your fault. By saying, *I Am Sorry,* you take responsibility for the hurt you caused. Sometimes the fault lies on both sides. Forgiveness needs to be extended and received to restore love and harmony. Being mutually healed is worth the awkwardness.

You will continue to make mistakes, and sometimes you don't realize that your actions cause emotional pain. When you offend someone, it is important to accept responsibility and apologize. The deeper the hurt, the longer the healing process. Often, you do something and don't think of its

REPERCUSSIONS FOR OTHERS. SAYING "I AM SORRY" OPENS THE DOOR TO COMMUNICATION AND BETTER UNDERSTANDING. AND IT SUGGESTS YOU WANT TO MAKE UP AND ASK FORGIVENESS. IT DOESN'T AUTOMATICALLY MEAN FORGIVENESS WILL FOLLOW. FORGIVENESS TAKES TIME. THE IMPACT OF OUR ACTIONS MAY HAVE LASTING EFFECTS.

FORGIVENESS IS WHAT YOU ARE ASKING FOR WHEN YOU APOLOGIZE. FIRST. YOU NEED TO FORGIVE YOURSELF. TO MAKE PEACE WITH YOURSELF. BY FORGIVING YOURSELF. YOU ARE NOT CLEARING YOURSELF OF BLAME BUT ACKNOWLEDGING THAT YOU DID WRONG. TAKING RESPONSIBILITY AND BEING SINCERELY SORRY IS ESSENTIAL TO FORGIVENESS.

EXPRESSING REGRET FOR WHAT YOU HAVE DONE IS THE BEGINNING OF BEING FORGIVEN. SOMETIMES WHAT YOU DID WAS AN OVERSIGHT AND UNINTENTIONAL. BUT IT CAUSED HURT AND DISAPPOINTMENT. BLAMING DOES NOT LEAD TO HEALING AND

> Saying 'I'm sorry'
> ' is saying 'I love you'
> with a wounded heart
> in one hand and your
> smothered pride
> in the other.
>
> Richelle E. Goodrich

FORGIVENESS. IGNORING THE ISSUE IS A BAD CHOICE. A SINCERE APOLOGY IS WELL RECEIVED MOST OF THE TIME. IT IS A REGRETFUL ACKNOWLEDGMENT. WITH A BRUISED HEART AND A DEFLATED EGO. HUMBLY EXPRESS YOUR SORROW AND ASK FORGIVENESS. AN APOLOGY IS ONLY THE BEGINNING. IT HELPS MEND BROKEN HEARTS AND RELATIONSHIPS AND SHOWS RESPECT AND EMPATHY TO THE WRONGED PERSON. THE EMOTIONAL BENEFITS ALLOW YOU TO MOVE PAST YOUR ANGER AND PREVENT YOU FROM BEING STUCK IN THE PAST. OPENING THE DOOR TO FORGIVENESS. AN APOLOGY REDUCES THE DEBILITATING EFFECTS OF REMORSE AND SHAME YOU MAY FEEL WHEN YOU HURT ANOTHER.

TWO SENTENCES ARE ESSENTIAL IN ANY RELATIONSHIP. "I AM SORRY. PLEASE FORGIVE ME. "I ONCE READ THE VULNERABLE SELF BELIEVES THE FIRST TO APOLOGIZE IS THE BRAVEST; THE FIRST TO FORGIVE IS THE STRONGEST; THE FIRST TO FORGET IS THE HAPPIEST. WHY IS IT SO HARD TO BE THE FIRST? A WISE PRACTICE IS TO FORGIVE

AND ASK FORGIVENESS BEFORE THE SUN SETS ON THE DAY. HARBORING HURTFUL FEELINGS PROLONGS THE AGONY AND DELAYS THE HEALING.

PONDER THIS THOUGHT: "IT TAKES A GREAT DEAL OF CHARACTER STRENGTH TO APOLOGIZE QUICKLY OUT OF ONE'S HEART RATHER THAN OUT OF PITY. A PERSON MUST POSSESS HIMSELF AND HAVE A DEEP SENSE OF SECURITY IN FUNDAMENTAL PRINCIPLES AND VALUES TO GENUINELY APOLOGIZE."

Stephen Covey

A GOOD HEART WON'T SETTLE UNTIL THINGS
ARE SET RIGHT AND TRUE.
SORRY DOESN'T TAKE THINGS BACK,
BUT IT PUSHED THINGS FORWARD.
IT BRIDGES THE GAP.
SORRY IS A SACRAMENT.
IT'S AN OFFERING. A GIFT.

Craig Silvey

DATE _____

LET YOUR HEART SPEAK

JOURNALING . . .

Valued and Treasured,
You Count!

THE AFFIRMING WORDS: *"YOU ARE THE MOST IMPORTANT PERSON IN MY LIFE. VERY SPECIAL TO MY HEART. I WILL CHERISH AND LOVE YOU FOREVER."* IS HEARTWARMING. YOU ARE VALUED. AND YOU COUNT. IN THE EYES OF ANOTHER. YOU ARE A TREASURE. THERE IS ONLY ONE OF YOU. AND YOU ARE BEAUTIFUL IN THE EYES OF YOUR BEHOLDER. AMAZINGLY. YOU COMPLETE SOMEONE ELSE'S STORY AND HAVE A REMARKABLE STORY OF YOUR OWN. YOU ARE YOUR KIND OF BEAUTIFUL. NOT EVERYONE WILL UNDERSTAND OR EVEN APPRECIATE YOU AS A WORK OF ART. BUT THOSE WHO DO WILL NEVER FORGET YOU AND VALUE YOU AS SOMEONE EXCEPTIONAL.

WHAT MAKES YOU VALUED? A GIFT FROM THE MOMENT OF CONCEPTION. YOU CAME INTO THE WORLD A BLESSING. YOU BROUGHT A UNIQUENESS NO ONE ELSE CAN GIVE. EVEN IN DIFFICULT TIMES. YOU LEFT YOUR MARK THROUGH ALL YOUR LIFE

EXPERIENCES. GOOD AND BAD. EVERY SUCCESS AND FAILURE. EVERY MOMENT OF STRENGTH AND WEAKNESS. KEEP THE FAITH! POPE FRANCIS TELLS US. *"HAVING FAITH DOES NOT MEAN HAVING NO DIFFICULTIES. BUT HAVING THE STRENGTH TO FACE THEM. KNOWING WE ARE NOT ALONE."* ALL YOU ARE. YOUR TALENTS. AND THE WISDOM YOU HAVE ACQUIRED MAKE YOU UNIQUE. YOUR EXPERIENCES HELP YOU DECIDE WHO JOURNEYS WITH YOU. HOW YOU SPEND YOUR TIME. AND WHAT YOU DEEM IMPORTANT. CARL JUNG FAMOUSLY SAID. *"YOU ARE WHAT YOU DO. NOT WHAT YOU SAY YOU'LL DO."*

YOUR VISION INFLUENCES WHAT YOU PERCEIVE AS BEAUTIFUL. NO ONE ELSE HAS LIVED YOUR TWENTY-FOUR-HOUR DAY EXCEPT YOU. ONLY YOU! YOU ARE ONE-OF-A-KIND. AND YOU RESPOND UNIQUELY TO LIFE'S HAPPENINGS. NO ONE ELSE SEES THE WORLD EXACTLY THE WAY YOU DO. SHARING YOUR WORLD PERCEPTIONS CAN UNLOCK PEARLS OF GREAT WISDOM FOR OTHERS. YOUR VALUES INFLUENCE YOUR CHOICES. TO EXPAND YOUR HORIZON. REACH OUT TO UNDERSTAND THE SUBTLE COMPLEXITIES OF OTHERS BY LISTENING INTENSELY TO THEIR UNIQUE STORIES.

YOUR GOALS AND AMBITIONS GUIDE HOW YOU SPEND YOUR TIME. ENERGY. AND EFFORT. YOUR PASSION IS PART OF WHAT MAKES YOU UNIQUE. UNDERSTANDING YOUR PASSION CAN HELP YOU FIND A PATH GUIDED BY YOUR VALUES AND PERCEPTIONS.

> **"**
> WORTHY NOW.
> NOT IF. NOT WHEN.
> WE ARE WORTHY OF
> LOVE
> AND BELONGING NOW.
> RIGHT THIS MINUTE.
> AS IS.
> *Brené Brown*
> **"**

NURTURE THE FLAME OF YOUR PASSION FOR KEEPING YOUR PURPOSE ALIVE AND LETTING YOUR CAUSE ILLUMINATE YOUR PATH. THERE IS NO DOUBT: YOU ARE AMAZING. IMPORTANT. AND VERY SPECIAL.

YOU ARE HERE FOR A GOOD REASON. YOU MAY NOT KNOW WHAT IT IS YET. BUT SOMEDAY IT WILL ALL MAKE SENSE TO YOU. IN THE MEANTIME. BELIEVE IN YOURSELF AND SHOW UP TO ACCOMPLISH THE ORDINARY WITH EXTRAORDINARY TOUCHES. LOVE WHO YOU CAN. HELP WHERE YOU CAN. AND GIVE WHAT YOU CAN.

It is good to ponder these questions: what makes you unique in this world from time to time? What are your passions and causes? What are the things that stir the most profound emotions in your soul?

As a person with gifts and talents, you have a responsibility to make a difference in the lives of others. You possess the greatest gift of all, the gift of affirming another. Use it to make someone else's life a little better. You live in a world that is not always kind. It is easy to forget the importance of others and your role in affirming their goodness. To validate others gives them the message that they count, they are important, and they matter. The beauty is that everyone is special. Aim to live in peace and harmony. You are not only responsible for yourself but also for the needs of others. Celebrate who you are and affirm the goodness of those around you.

Ponder this thought: "Be soft. Do not let the world make you hard. Do not let the pain make you hate. Do not let the bitterness steal your sweetness. Take pride that even though the rest of the world may disagree, you still believe it to be a beautiful place."

Kurt Vonnegut

Date _____

LET YOUR HEART SPEAK

JOURNALING . . .

WELLNESS:
THE MIND-BODY-SPIRIT CONNECTION

THE MIND-BODY-SPIRIT CONNECTION DESCRIBES THE THREE ENTWINED ASPECTS OF BEING HUMAN. THE PHYSICAL, MENTAL, AND SPIRITUAL COMBINE TO MAKE YOU HOLISTICALLY WHO YOU ARE. THE MIND IS NOT SEPARATE FROM THE BODY. MIND, BODY, AND SPIRIT ARE BEAUTIFULLY INTERLINKED. THESE THREE PILLARS INSPIRE AND INFORM YOUR EXPERIENCES. SEEING YOURSELF AS AN INTEGRATED WHOLE INSTEAD OF A CONGLOMERATE OF PARTS IS THE CORE COMPONENT OF HOLISTIC HEALING. THE NEED TO CARE FOR YOUR WHOLE SELF BECOMES APPARENT. WHEN YOU LOVE AND CARE FOR YOURSELF - MIND, BODY, AND SPIRIT - YOUR WHOLE SELF WORKS IN HARMONY.

MIND, BODY, AND SPIRIT MEAN THAT YOUR WELL-BEING COMES FROM PHYSICAL, MENTAL, AND SPIRITUAL HEALTH. TO BE *"HEALTHY,"* YOU ARE CALLED TO PAY

ATTENTION TO ALL THREE OF THESE ASPECTS. YOU ARE MORE THAN JUST YOUR THOUGHTS.

YOUR MENTAL HEALTH PARTLY DETERMINES YOUR PHYSICAL HEALTH. IT IS COMMON TODAY THAT MEDICAL DOCTORS ASK YOU ABOUT STRESS AND TURMOIL IN YOUR LIFE WHEN YOU SEE THEM FOR PHYSICAL AILMENTS. THAT'S BECAUSE THEY KNOW TO PAY ATTENTION TO THE MIND-BODY-SPIRIT CONNECTION.

PSYCHIATRISTS AND THERAPISTS BELIEVE PEOPLE WHO HARBOR NEGATIVE EMOTIONS CAN OFTEN MAKE THEMSELVES PHYSICALLY SICK. LIKEWISE. MENTAL HEALTH ISSUES CAN MANIFEST THEMSELVES IN THE BODY. CAUSING DISEASE. YOUR BODY IS A BAROMETER THAT INDICATES HOW THINGS ARE GOING IN ALL AREAS. IT ALSO PROVIDES THE MUSCULOSKELETAL STRUCTURE AND THE VITAL TISSUES AND ORGANS THAT CARRY

YOU THROUGH THIS LIFE. TRUE HEALTH/WELLNESS COMES WHEN YOU CREATE HARMONY AND BALANCE AMONG ALL PARTS—

TAKING TIME TO TEND TO YOURSELF AS A WHOLE PERSON CAN OPEN ENERGY CHANNELS. THESE CONNECTIONS CONTRIBUTE TO YOUR SPIRITUALLY SOUND. MENTALLY STIMULATING. EMOTIONALLY CENTERED. VIBRANT LIFE. LISTEN TO YOUR EMOTIONAL AND SPIRITUAL NEEDS AS YOU SEEK GREATER HAPPINESS. JOY. HEALTH. AND FULFILLMENT. BY PAYING ATTENTION TO MIND-BODY-SPIRIT COMPONENTS. YOU ARE ON YOUR WAY TO A MORE BALANCED SELF. BECCA LEE ELOQUENTLY STATES: *IF YOU SEEK PEACE. BE STILL. IF YOU SEEK WISDOM. BE SILENT. IF YOU SEEK LOVE. BE YOURSELF.*

> CREATE
> BALANCE.
> NURTURE YOUR SOUL.
> FEED YOUR BODY.
> EXPAND YOUR MIND.
> STRENGHTEN
> YOURSELF.
> *Anonymous*

BECAUSE OF THE PANDEMIC STRESSORS. IT BECAME NECESSARY FOR MANY TO RESORT TO BETTER WELLNESS CARE AND IMPLEMENT AT-HOME ROUTINES TO ATTEMPT SOME RESEMBLANCE OF CALM AND PEACE.

IT IS IMPORTANT TO EXERCISE HEALTHY HABITS DAILY TO ATTAIN BETTER PHYSICAL AND MENTAL HEALTH OUTCOMES SO THAT INSTEAD OF JUST SURVIVING. YOU

ARE THRIVING. WELLNESS IS THE HARMONIOUS CONNECTION OF THE MIND. BODY. AND SPIRIT - NOT MERELY THE ABSENCE OF DISEASE. THEREFORE. SIMPLE AND HEALTHY CHANGES TO YOUR LIFESTYLE WILL HELP IMPROVE YOUR *QUALITY OF LIFE.*

CHANCES ARE. IF YOU LOOK AT YOUR BELIEF SYSTEM. YOU WILL FIND BITS AND PIECES OF THE MIND-BODY-SPIRIT CONNECTION ALREADY IN PLACE. TODAY. IT IS COMMON TO COMBINE A FAITH WALK. EXERCISES IN SPIRITUALITY AND MEDIATION. A HEALTHY DIET. AND ALTERNATIVE MEDICINE AS A PLAN FOR HEALING HOLISTIC LIVING. A YOGA CLASS COMPLEMENTS YOUR PSYCHOANALYST SESSION. AS DOES YOUR MORNING RUN. YOUR MEDITATION. YOUR VEGAN DIET. OR EVEN YOUR WEEKLY VISITS TO THE SPA. EXPERIENCE THE FREEDOM OF CHOOSING THE ACTIVITIES THAT HELP YOU LIVE HOLISTICALLY - MIND. BODY. AND SPIRIT. TAKE IT SLOW AND GIVE YOUR BODY A CHANCE TO CATCH UP WITH YOUR MIND AND SPIRIT. BE PROUD OF HOW HARD YOU ARE TRYING. MAY YOU KNOW THE BLESSING OF GOD. PEACEFULLY GUIDING YOU THROUGH CHALLENGING TIMES WITH THE EASE OF A GRACEFUL DANCER GLIDING IN MIDAIR. BE WELL!

PONDER THIS THOUGHT: "EVERY EXPERIENCE. NO MATTER HOW BAD IT SEEMS. HOLDS WITHIN IT A BLESSING OF SOME KIND. THE GOAL IS TO FIND IT. "

Buddha

DATE _____

LET YOUR HEART SPEAK

JOURNALING . . .

XOXO: HUGS AND KISSES

AFTER MORE THAN A YEAR OF ISOLATION, WE WELCOME THE WARMTH OF AN EMBRACE. HUGS AND KISSES ARE OUTWARD SIGNS OF LOVE AND AFFECTION. I'M SURE YOU'VE SEEN PEOPLE SIGN LETTERS, CARDS, EMAILS, OR TEXT MESSAGES WITH XO, MEANING *HUGS AND KISSES.* IT HAS BECOME A FAMOUS SIGNATORY STATEMENT.

> A HUG IS A
> GREAT GIFT.
> ONE SIZE FITS ALL,
> AND IT IS EASY TO
> EXCHANGE.
> *Anonymous*

BEING DENIED CLOSENESS DURING THE PANDEMIC HAS BEEN DIFFICULT. IT HAS BEEN ESPECIALLY DIFFICULT FOR GRANDPARENTS WHO HAVEN'T BEEN ABLE TO EMBRACE THEIR GRANDCHILDREN. THE VACCINE IS A SIGN OF HOPE FOR REUNITING AND EMBRACING SAFELY. THE LACK OF HUGS AND KISSES CREATED A VOID AND ROBBED US OF THE EMOTIONAL

CONNECTIONS VITAL TO OUR WELL-BEING. THE ISOLATION AND LONELINESS HAVE BEEN SOME OF THE MOST STRESSFUL PARTS OF THE PANDEMIC.

TOUCH IS THE FIRST SENSE WE ACQUIRE. OUR FIRST LANGUAGE. SOMETIMES WE NEED TO PAUSE AND REGAIN FLUENCY IN OUR FIRST LANGUAGE. YET. TOUCH IS ESSENTIAL TO THRIVING. NOW. MORE THAN EVER. WE NOTICE HUMAN TOUCH IN A WAY THAT WE DIDN'T BEFORE THE PANDEMIC. BLOWING A KISS OR WAVING GOODBYE IS NOT THE SAME AS A PHYSICAL EMBRACE. TOUCH IS HOW WE FIRST COMMUNICATE AS BABIES AND IS FUNDAMENTAL TO OUR WELL-BEING ALL THE YEARS OF OUR LIVES. IT IS A NATURAL PHENOMENON TO TOUCH AND BE TOUCHED. THE NEED FOR TOUCH EXISTS BELOW THE HORIZON OF CONSCIOUSNESS. BEING DEPRIVED OF TOUCH LIMITS OUR COMMUNICATION. TOUCH HAS A SIGNIFICANT IMPACT ON OUR PSYCHOLOGICAL AND PHYSICAL WELL-BEING. EMBRACING OUR CLOSE FRIENDS AND FAMILY IS A BLESSING BEYOND MEASURE.

DACHER KELTNER. A UNIVERSITY OF CALIFORNIA. BERKELEY SOCIOLOGIST WHO STUDIES THE IMPACT OF TOUCH. IS CONCERNED ABOUT SOCIAL DISTANCING'S LONG-TERM IMPLICATIONS. HE SAYS THAT EVEN THE SLIGHTEST PHYSICAL CONTACT HOLDS TOGETHER THE FABRIC OF SOCIETY. *"TOUCH IS AS IMPORTANT A SOCIAL CONDITION AS ANYTHING."* KELTNER SAYS. *"IT REDUCES STRESS. HELPING PEOPLE TO TRUST ONE ANOTHER. WHEN YOU FEEL LONELY. YOU RUN THE RISK OF STRESS. ADD TO THAT THE QUARANTINE. AND THAT ELEVATES THE SEVERITY."*

A WARM EMBRACE HAS MANY BENEFITS. THERAPEUTICALLY AFFECTING THE MIND. BODY. AND SPIRIT. AN EMBRACE MEANS CLOSENESS AND IS THE MOST INTIMATE EXPRESSION OF LOVE. IT REINFORCES CONNECTIONS. PROVIDES A SENSE OF SAFETY. AND IMPROVES THE INTENSITY OF YOUR UNDERSTANDING OF BELONGING TO ANOTHER. AN EMBRACE IS A FORM OF COMMUNICATION THAT ALLOWS YOU TO EXPRESS THINGS YOU CANNOT PUT INTO WORDS. EMBRACING CALMS YOU. FOR A FEW MOMENTS. YOU CAN FORGET THE PROBLEMS THAT STRESS YOU. IT HELPS YOU OVERCOME FEAR. TO GIVE AND RECEIVE AN EMBRACE SOOTHES YOUR SOUL AND THE SOUL OF ANOTHER. HUGS HAVE BEEN SHOWN TO ENHANCE OXYTOCIN LEVELS AND HELP ALLEVIATE FEELINGS OF LONELINESS. BOREDOM. ISOLATION. ANGER. AND OTHER NEGATIVE EMOTIONS. AN EXTENDED EMBRACE RAISES SEROTONIN LEVELS. WHICH CAN IMPROVE YOUR MOOD AND QUALITY OF LIFE WHILE ALSO RELAXING YOUR MUSCLES AND

RELIEVING STRESS. FEEL FREE TO GIVE A HUG. IT IS FREE FOR THE GIVING BUT HAS PRICELESS BENEFITS.

It's the little things in life that go a long way when it comes to showing those dearest to you how much you love and care. So be generous with your hugs and kisses, and embrace more. The human connection is life-giving and healing. Hugs are both a way to celebrate and provide comfort without saying a single word. There are many reasons to give a hug, but no explanation is needed. Help another thrive; give a hug, a loving embrace.

Ponder this thought: "I will not play tug o' war. I'd rather play hug o' war. Where everyone hugs instead of tugs. Where everyone giggles and rolls on the rug. Where everyone kisses. And everyone grins. And everyone cuddles. And everyone wins."

Margo Georgiadis

Hugs

A hug shows someone how much you care —

You can give a hug anytime & anywhere.

Being gentle and kind is where you start —

Because when you do that

You hug a heart.

DATE

LET YOUR HEART SPEAK

JOURNALING . . .

YES to Intentional Living

W E HUNGER FOR A GREATER PURPOSE AND THE CHANCE TO CREATE POSITIVE CHANGE IN THE WORLD. IN RECENT YEARS, INTENTIONAL LIVING SEEMS TO BE THE BUZZWORD. BUT WHAT DOES IT MEAN? DO YOU EVER GET A FEELING SOMETHING ISN'T RIGHT? DO YOU EVER FEEL YOU ARE LIVING ON AUTOPILOT? WHEN YOU LIVE IN A CONSTANT STATE OF OVERWHELM, YOU TEND TO OVERTHINK AND STRESS ABOUT INSIGNIFICANT DETAILS. TO LIVE INTENTIONALLY IS TO LIVE WITH A SENSE OF DIRECTION AND PURPOSE. LIVING WITH INTENTION MEANS CHOOSING THE PATH THAT BEST WORKS FOR YOU AND YOUR LIFESTYLE. INTENTIONAL LIVING HELPS YOU SET A COURSE FOR YOUR LIFE RATHER THAN AIMLESSLY WANDERING THROUGH IT. SOME INTENTIONAL LIVING EXAMPLES INCLUDE CO-HOUSING, ETHICAL LIVING, FRUGAL LIVING, SIMPLE LIVING, AND SUSTAINABLE LIVING. OR, IT CAN BE AS SIMPLE AS DECIDING TO EXERCISE DAILY AND TAKING PERSONAL TIME TO MEDITATE.

The goal is simply to live your life with a purpose. It is about the "Whys" and then accepting the answers. The transformative practice of intention can help you discover a radically different, gratifying way of life. An intentional approach questions how you live authentically.

You cannot avoid all failures, but you can become more intentional about dealing with your mistakes. Failures are pauses. Don't let failures be the reason to give up on your goal to achieve intentional living. As you become more comfortable and confident with making intentional choices and being mindful of your world, you will become aware of who you are and what you want from life. You can build a more meaningful life, which may be the most rewarding thing you've ever done. One change won't take care of all the issues in your life, but it will give you one thing to focus on and feel more intentional about every day. Intentional living is about choosing to do something new and different and committing to it. Sometimes risks are what it takes to fulfill your dreams.

Try to be more intentional today. Choose to live, not merely to exist. Choosing to live with intention is not only about the destination, but about every path, detour, and respite of life's journey. You can start by listening to your inner voice. Starting over is sometimes necessary when you decide to live intentionally. You may discover you have been pursuing the wrong path and opt to start from scratch. It is never too late to change course. Taking a different path at any age can be rejuvenating, empowering, and life-giving. The by-product is that you

66

Be the change
you wish
to see
in the world.

Mahatma Gandhi

99

can be happier and more fulfilled. Most of us are not seeking a perfect life but desire a happy life. Choose intentionally to live the happy life you desire. Deep within the recesses of your being, you know what path you need to take to find your way to happiness and peace. Be still and listen!

Journaling is an excellent way to keep track of your goals. You can keep a record of your feelings and the challenges and obstacles you

ENCOUNTER. BEGIN SLOWLY AND TAKE SMALL STEPS. PACE YOURSELF UNTIL YOU CAN SEE A DIFFERENCE. BE PATIENT! IT TAKES TIME. STAY THE COURSE. THE REWARD FOR BUILDING A BETTER LIFE IS PEACE AND CONTENTMENT. WHAT MATTERS IS DECIDING WHAT YOU ARE DOING AND WHY YOU ARE DOING IT. NOT JUST GOING WHERE LIFE TAKES YOU. BUILD YOUR BEST LIFE! STRIVE TO BE HAPPY!

PONDER THIS THOUGHT: "LEARN TO BE WHAT YOU ARE. AND LEARN TO RESIGN WITH A GOOD GRACE ALL THAT YOU ARE NOT."

Henri Frederic Amiel

DATE _____

LET YOUR HEART SPEAK

JOURNALING . . .

BELIEVE
THERE IS
GOOD
IN THIS
WORLD.

Be the good!

ZERO IN ON BEING THE GOOD

THE PAST FEW YEARS HAVE BEEN VOLATILE IN MANY WAYS. FAKE NEWS NEVER FADED. MISTRUST, DESTRUCTIVE BEHAVIORS, DISREGARD FOR LIFE, RACIAL BRUTALITY, AND ESCALATING VIOLENCE SEEMED TO DOMINATE THE NEWS. IT IS EASY TO LOSE PERSPECTIVE AND BEGIN TO DOUBT, BE ANGRY, ANXIOUS, AND FEARFUL. YET, WE NEED TO BELIEVE THERE IS PLENTY OF GOOD IN THIS WORLD OF OURS. CARING PEOPLE HAVE REACHED OUT IN KINDNESS, LOVE, AND CONCERN. AS SMALL AS IT MAY APPEAR, SMILING EVEN WHILE WEARING A MASK ACKNOWLEDGES A HUMAN CONNECTION. SMILING HAS REPLACED TOUCH AND SENDS THE MESSAGE, *"I NOTICE YOU, AND I WISH YOU WELL."* WE CONTINUE TO BE INSPIRED BY THE LITTLE ACTS OF KINDNESS AND THE COURAGEOUS WITNESSING OF COMPASSION. THESE ARE THE THINGS THAT TOUCH OUR HEARTS AND FILL US WITH HOPE.

THE BAG OF COOKIES OR LOAF OF HOMEMADE BREAD LEFT AT THE DOOR WITH A NOTE SAYING, *"I AM THINKING OF YOU,"* THE WELLNESS CHECK CALL, THE INVISIBLE SMILE BENEATH THE MASK DETECTED BY A TWINKLE IN THE EYE, DO NOT MAKE THE HEADLINES. MAX ERHMAN, IN 1927, WROTE THE DESIDERATA (THE LATIN WORD FOR

DESIRE.) IT CONTAINS AN INSPIRING MESSAGE OF HOPE RELEVANT TODAY AS THE CORONAVIRUS CONTINUES TO INSTILL FEAR AND RESTLESSNESS IN THE HEARTS OF MANY.

BELIEVE THERE IS GOOD IN THIS WORLD. AND KNOW YOU ARE THE REASON FOR THE GOOD. WHEN YOU SHOW UP AND BE THE GOOD BY BEING YOU AND LIVING YOUR AUTHENTIC SELF. YOU INFLUENCE OTHERS TO DO THE SAME. AS A SOCIAL BEING. WHAT YOU DO AND HOW YOU ACT IMPACT OTHERS. YOUR KINDNESS CAN MOTIVATE OTHERS TO BE KIND AND REACH OUT TO OFFER HELP. YOUR BELIEFS. ATTITUDES. FEELINGS. AND ACTIONS AFFECT THOSE AROUND YOU. BE THE GOOD BY SPREADING GOODNESS TO OTHERS AND INSPIRING OTHERS TO MAKE A DIFFERENCE. IT HAS A RIPPLE EFFECT. INSPIRE OTHERS TO BE THE GOOD. THE GREATEST GIFT YOU CAN GIVE THE WORLD IS TO LEAD BY EXAMPLE. SHOW UP AS YOUR VERY BEST. AND GO AFTER YOUR PURPOSE WITH PERSISTENCE. BECAUSE WHEN YOU DO THAT. YOU WILL MOTIVATE OTHERS TO DO THE SAME. DO NOT ASK WHAT THIS WORLD HAS TO OFFER YOU. BUT INSTEAD WHAT YOU HAVE TO OFFER THIS WORLD. BE THE GOOD IN THIS WORLD. IT IS THE MOST REWARDING WAY TO APPROACH LIFE. AND YOU MIGHT CHANGE SOMEONE'S LIFE. YES. THERE IS GOOD IN THIS WORLD. AND YOU ARE CALLED TO BE THE GOOD — THE DESIDERATA – WORDS OF HOPE FOR LIFE.

DESIDERATA

by Max Erhmam, 1927

GO PLACIDLY AMID THE NOISE AND HASTE.
AND REMEMBER WHAT PEACE THERE MAY BE IN SILENCE.
AS FAR AS POSSIBLE WITHOUT SURRENDER
BE ON GOOD TERMS WITH ALL PERSONS.
SPEAK YOUR TRUTH QUIETLY AND CLEARLY.
AND LISTEN TO OTHERS.

EVEN THE DULL AND THE IGNORANT;
THEY, TOO, HAVE THEIR STORY.

AVOID LOUD AND AGGRESSIVE PERSONS.
THEY ARE VEXATIONS TO THE SPIRIT.
IF YOU COMPARE YOURSELF WITH OTHERS,
YOU MAY BECOME VAIN AND BITTER;
FOR ALWAYS THERE WILL BE GREATER AND LESSER PERSONS
THAN YOURSELF.
ENJOY YOUR ACHIEVEMENTS AS WELL AS YOUR PLANS.

KEEP INTERESTED IN YOUR OWN CAREER, HOWEVER HUMBLE;
IT IS A REAL POSSESSION IN THE CHANGING FORTUNES OF TIME.
EXERCISE CAUTION IN YOUR BUSINESS AFFAIRS;
FOR THE WORLD IS FULL OF TRICKERY.
BUT LET THIS NOT BLIND YOU TO WHAT VIRTUE THERE IS;
MANY PERSONS STRIVE FOR HIGH IDEALS;
AND EVERYWHERE LIFE IS FULL OF HEROISM.

BE YOURSELF. NEITHER BE CYNICAL ABOUT LOVE;
FOR IN THE FACE OF ALL ARIDITY AND DISENCHANTMENT
IT IS AS PERENNIAL AS THE GRASS.
TAKE KINDLY THE COUNSEL OF THE YEARS,
GRACEFULLY SURRENDERING THE THINGS OF YOUTH.
NURTURE STRENGTH OF SPIRIT TO SHIELD YOU
BUT DO NOT DISTRESS YOURSELF WITH DARK IMAGININGS.
MANY FEARS ARE BORN OF FATIGUE AND LONELINESS.
BEYOND A WHOLESOME DISCIPLINE,
BE GENTLE WITH YOURSELF.
YOU ARE A CHILD OF THE UNIVERSE,
NO LESS THAN THE TREES AND THE STARS;

You have a right to be here.
And whether or not it is clear to you.
No doubt the universe is unfolding as it should.
Therefore be at peace with God.
whatever you conceive Him to be.
and whatever your labors and aspirations.
In the noisy confusion of life keep peace with your soul.

With all its sham. drudgery. and broken dreams.
It is still a beautiful world.
Be cheerful. Strive to be happy.

DATE _____

LET YOUR HEART SPEAK

JOURNALING . . .

As the sun sets on another day . . .

May you know God's peace.

Epilogue

THE PANDEMIC OFFERED ME QUIET TIME WITHOUT INTERRUPTIONS TO WORK ON THIS BOOK. WOVEN THROUGHOUT THE REFLECTIONS ARE VALUES AND PHILOSOPHIES TO INSPIRE AND GUIDE YOU. I HOPE THEY WILL BE THOUGHT-PROVOKING AS WELL AS A CHANNEL FOR GREATER MEANING AND PURPOSE IN YOUR LIFE.

WHILE WORKING AS A BEREAVEMENT THERAPIST AND HOSPICE CHAPLAIN, I HAD THE PRIVILEGE OF JOURNEYING WITH THE DYING DURING THE LAST FEW WEEKS AND DAYS OF THEIR LIVES. THESE ENCOUNTERS CAUSED ME TO QUESTION MY MORTALITY AND THE MANY MYSTERIES OF LIFE. BECAUSE DEATH WAS A FREQUENT OCCURRENCE, I OFTEN GOT LOST IN THE PAIN AND ANGUISH OF THE DYING AND THEIR GRIEVING LOVED ONES. WITNESSING HUMANITY'S RAWNESS AFFECTED MY EMOTIONAL EQUILIBRIUM. OUR HISTORY OF LIVED EXPERIENCES SHAPES OUR PERSPECTIVE ON LIFE SITUATIONS. OUR LIVES' JOURNEYS SEEM TO BE THE BLENDING OF CELEBRATION AND GRIEF AND EVERYTHING IN BETWEEN.

LIFE HAS TAUGHT ME I AM NOT ALWAYS IN CONTROL. LIFE IS FULL OF EXPERIENCES, LESSONS, HEARTBREAK, AND PAIN. BUT IT HAS ALSO SHOWN ME THE

POSITIVE IMPACT OF LOVE, BEAUTY, POSSIBILITY, AND THE GIFT OF NEW BEGINNINGS. As I try to embrace all of life, my desire to be uniquely me gives me the resolve to embrace each new day with hope in my heart. My lived experiences have changed me. I cannot go back to the person I once was. I can only go forward and continue to embark on a new day with my history and wisdom as a guide. It is my challenge to live my ordinary life with extraordinary intentions.

Rachel Marie Martin so brilliantly states, *"An extraordinary life doesn't need to be filled with just accomplishments. An extraordinary life is often found in the simplest of moments – times of love, of courage, of empathy, of simply being there for each other. Truly the ordinary is often the most extraordinary."*

As I reflected on my life's journey, I envisioned it as an excursion mapped out with a AAA TripTik. My destination stops were blessings in disguise. I traveled up and down the east coast from New England to Florida with a teaching stint in St. Croix. Before retiring, I spent nine years working with the good people in the Appalachia's foothills in Kentucky. It was a special detour inland, rich with blessings.

While in Kentucky, I had the good fortune of working with the administrative team at Our Lady of Bellefonte Hospital. Our CEO, Kevin Halter, taught me many valuable lessons. His work ethic, dedication, inclusivity, and ability to empower our team were remarkable. I witnessed the compassion and kindness of the medical staff, treating patients with the kind-heartedness they would show to their loved ones.

My TripTik has been restricted these past few years due to the pandemic. During the isolation phase of COVID-19, I took an inward excursion to reflect on my life experiences and appreciate the meaning and purpose of my existence. With the gift of time, I questioned and discovered a lot about myself as I listened to the inner voice of my heart. This retreat experience highlighted the highs and lows of my life. I have a deeper appreciation for those who accompanied me along the way and helped me

CULTIVATE THE SEEDS OF GRATITUDE. LIFE IS A GIFT THAT WE HAVE ONE CHANCE AT LIVING.

It has been forty years since my life-threatening ovarian cancer diagnosis, and I still wear my anchor necklace. And I still cling to it when I am struggling, confused, or fearful. I have been so blessed. In 1981, I prayed to God for just one more year. On Christmas morning of that year, my sister Ann hugged me and wished me a Merry Christmas. I remember breaking into tears and crying, *"But I want to be here next Christmas."* My anchor necklace has served as a tangible reminder that God journeys with me during the good and challenging times. Even when I doubted God, God never abandoned me.

As you come to the end of this book, I wish you a beautiful *quality of life* all your days. I hope the reflections have helped you choose to live your best life. Listen to your inner voice and follow the urgings of your heart. Go forward with a greater appreciation of the little things in life that matter the most. And, as you live your intentional life, be patient and trust the process. What is important will be revealed in God's good time. Slow down and be still remembering the words of Robin Williams: *"Everyone you meet is fighting a battle you know nothing about. Be kind. Always."*

Life is short, regardless of how many years we have on this earth. But it is not about the number of your years and very much about the quality of your years. Strive to live in peace and harmony. Cherish all the blessings in your life, be patient during the frustrating times. Reach out in loving support to those in need. Your presence is the most precious gift to those alone in their pain. Believe you deserve a good life and approach life with a positive outlook. You reap what you sow.

St. Francis de Sales wrote a prayer of consolation and peace. During times of struggle and when you are weary with worry, *"Be at peace and put aside all anxious thoughts and imaginations."* So often, our fearful imaginings are only that – imaginations. Take it a day at a time. You can live with uncertainty for a time as you pray for discernment and guidance.

Mornings seem to forgive the fearful dread of the night, giving way to a
new day filled with renewed hope.
Be at peace!

Prayer of St. Francis de Sales

DO NOT LOOK FORWARD
TO WHAT MIGHT HAPPEN TOMORROW.
THE SAME EVERLASTING GOD
WHO CARES FOR YOU TODAY
WILL CARE FOR YOU TOMORROW
AND EVERY DAY.
EITHER GOD WILL SHIELD YOU
FROM SUFFERING
OR GIVE YOU THE UNFAILING STRENGTH
TO BEAR IT.

Be at peace,

AND PUT ASIDE

all anxious thoughts

and imaginations.

The Gift of NOW

Take the time to slow down and
intentionally pause to discover

the gift of the present moment.

Do not be in a rush and miss out on

the blessings of this moment,

this day.

Anchor yourself and stay focused on the
here and now.

Enjoy the view.

Let the beauty of the universe

soothe your soul,

nurture your spirit.

May God's love be your guide as you pause
to count your blessings and

celebrate the gift of NOW.

Life is precious.

MPG

Never doubt . . .

You are special.

You count!

Acknowledgments

HOW DO I SAY *"THANK YOU"* TO ALL THOSE WHO HAVE TOUCHED MY LIFE AND EMPOWERED ME TO GROW IN WISDOM AND GRACE AND TO KEEP GOING WHEN I FELL SHORT OF MY EXPECTATIONS? FIRST, I AM MOST GRATEFUL TO MY LOVED ONES AND DEAR FRIENDS WHO ENCOURAGED ME TO DREAM IMPOSSIBLE DREAMS AND CHASE AFTER THEM WITH DETERMINATION AND PERSEVERANCE. NEXT, I TENDER MY GRATITUDE TO FR. THOMAS J. DONELLAN AND SISTER PATRICIA GAMGORT, OSB, FOR THEIR LOVE, GUIDANCE, AND FRIENDSHIP SINCE MY CHILDHOOD YEARS. DURING MY YOUTH, THEY WERE A BLESSING AND HAVE BEEN A SUPPORTIVE PRESENCE IN MY ADULT LIFE.

MY FOUR NEPHEWS AND THEIR FAMILIES HOLD A SPECIAL PLACE IN MY HEART. THROUGH THE YEARS, FAMILY AND FRIENDS HAVE POSITIVELY INFLUENCED THE EBBS AND FLOWS OF THE RHYTHMICAL PATTERNS OF MY LIFE. GOD PUT GOOD PEOPLE IN MY LIFE FOR A REASON, TRAVERSING MANY SEASONS. I AM GRATEFUL FOR THE FRIENDSHIPS THAT HAVE BLOSSOMED THROUGH THE YEARS. EACH FRIEND SUPPORTED ME DURING AN IMPORTANT PHASE, PASSING THE TORCH TO ANOTHER AS I VENTURED ONWARD ON THIS SACRED AND AMAZING JOURNEY CALLED LIFE.

As a college student, I benefited from outstanding professors at Notre Dame of Maryland University. Sister Virgina Geiger, SSND, a professor in the philosophy department, was one of the many exceptional faculty members. We stayed in touch over the decades. Sister gently challenged me to follow my dreams. Toward the end of her life, I was her hospice chaplain and had the privilege of spending time with Sister during her last days and was grateful to visit her a few hours before her death. With tears, I thanked her for the precious gift of her friendship. I may not recall the basics of logic, metaphysics, or epistemology, but I will never forget Sister Virgina's genuine interest, loving-kindness, and encouraging words.

Even at a young age, my mother often said to me, *"You go where angels fear to tread."* That has been true on many levels, a theme woven throughout my life's journey. I am a lover of wonder and awe, always believing there is more to life than the obvious. My mother knew my heart. She worried for my safety because I had no fear and was willing to take risks, even when danger was lurking.

I am grateful to Gilchrist, a hospice service in Maryland, for the privilege of being part of the chaplaincy team. As chaplains, we ministered to the seriously ill and end-of-life patients and their families. The dying taught me precious lessons about living and treasuring the gift of life.

Blessed am I with great memories of my students, from grade school children to young adults in graduate school. Their innocence, goodness, and enthusiasm to make the world a better place made teaching so rewarding.

Those I had the privilege of counseling touched my heart with their honesty and humility as they searched for meaning and purpose. They taught me that, in some fashion, we are all bent but not broken.

With heartfelt appreciation, I am grateful to the Sisters of Bon Secours. My family's connection with the Sisters dates back to 1918. That year, my father was a young child when a house fire severely injured him a few blocks from the Bon Secours Hospital's building site. He had the

HIGHEST ESTEEM FOR THE TWO SISTERS WHO, FOR MONTHS, PROVIDED HOME HEALTH CARE AND NURSED HIM BACK TO HEALTH. HE NEVER FORGOT THEIR LOVING KINDNESS. IT WAS MY HOPE TO ONE DAY BECOME A PART OF THE SISTERS OF BON SECOURS' MINISTRY. MY DREAM BECAME A REALITY IN 2009 WHEN I JOINED THE ADMINISTRATIVE TEAM AT OUR LADY OF BELLEFONTE HOSPITAL IN ASHLAND, KENTUCKY, AN AFFILIATE OF THE BON SECOURS HEALTH SYSTEM. DURING MY NINE YEARS IN ASHLAND, KENTUCKY, SISTER ANNE LUTZ, CBS, SERVED AS THE CHIEF SPONSORSHIP OFFICER FOR BON SECOURS HEALTH SYSTEM. A HUMBLE AND WISE LEADER, SISTER ANNE WAS THE EPITOME OF A CALMING PRESENCE IN THE SOMETIMES ANXIOUS WORKPLACE. SISTER ANNE HAS BEEN AN INSPIRATION TO ALL WHO WERE PRIVILEGED TO BE MENTORED BY HER.

WHILE IN KENTUCKY, I WITNESSED THE DEDICATED LEADERSHIP AND THE KIND-HEARTED WORK OF CARING PHYSICIANS, NURSES, AND STAFF DOING GOD'S HEALING WORK EVERY DAY AS THEY LIVED THE BON SECOURS MISSION AND VALUES. SADLY, OUR LADY OF BELLEFONTE HOSPITAL CLOSED IN APRIL 2020. I AM SURE THAT BEAUTIFUL PLACE ON THE HILL WILL ECHO MEMORIES OF COMPASSIONATE CARE DELIVERED WITH AMAZING GRACE FOR DECADES TO COME.

"Peace I leave you;

my peace I give to you;

not as the world gives

do I give to you?

Do not let your heart

be troubled,

nor let it be fearful."

John 14:27

About the Author

MARGUERITE PATRICIA WRITES FROM THE SOUTHERN SHORE OF DELAWARE, WHERE THE TRANQUIL BEACHES ECHO THE PEACE AND CALM SHE PROMOTES IN HER BOOKS. SHE GREW UP IN ILCHESTER, ON THE OUTSKIRTS OF ELLICOTT CITY, MARYLAND. SHE RETIRED TO DELAWARE IN 2018.

MARGUERITE PATRICIA RECEIVED HER BACHELOR'S DEGREE FROM THE NOW NOTRE DAME OF MARYLAND UNIVERSITY AND HAS GRADUATE DEGREES FROM LOYOLA UNIVERSITY OF MARYLAND, THE JOHNS HOPKINS UNIVERSITY, AND THE GEORGE WASHINGTON UNIVERSITY. SHE STUDIED ART DESIGN AT BARRY UNIVERSITY IN MIAMI SHORES, FLORIDA.

BEFORE RETIRING, MARGUERITE'S CAREER INCLUDED WORKING AS A LICENSED THERAPIST, CHAPLAIN, EDUCATOR, AND HEALTHCARE PROFESSIONAL. HER MINISTRY GOALS WERE TO ADVOCATE FOR PATIENT RIGHTS, ENDORSE PALLIATIVE END-OF-LIFE CARE AND IMPROVE THE *QUALITY OF LIFE* FOR THOSE SUFFERING FROM CHRONIC, MENTAL, AND TERMINAL ILLNESSES. HER PASSION FOR PROMOTING QUALITY LIVING IS EVIDENT IN HER WRITINGS.

"Look to the birds of the air...
They do not sow or reap, yet their
Heavenly Father feeds them."
Luke 12

"Consider the lilies of the field and how they grow.
They neither toil nor spin.
Are you not of more value than they?"
Matthew 6

Be still . . .

as you listen

to your HEART.

Stay anchored in HOPE.

Take Gentle Care.

HONEYSUCKLE HILL PUBLISHING

MILTON, DELAWARE

Made in the USA
Middletown, DE
11 March 2022

62472802R00106